D. Caroline Coile, Ph.D.

American Eskimo Dogs

Everything About Purchase, Care, Nutrition, Behavior, and Training

Filled with Full-color Photographs

Illustrations by Michele Earle-Bridges

BARRON'S

THE EVOLVING ESKIE

The enigmatic Eskie—a breed both rare and familiar, ancient and modern—is a breed of such undeniable appeal that its cuteness has been described as its major flaw.

Circus dog, farm dog, watchdog, even draft dog—the American Eskimo Dog's original role is not clear. But one thing never disputed is that the American Eskimo Dog ("Eskie" to its friends) is a companion dog par excellence.

Although the American Eskimo Dog will gladly chase marauding squirrels, will gleefully give its best at pulling a sled, and will ball up on any family member's lap without hesitation, its popularity cannot be traced to only one role. Though documentation about the breed's origins is obscure, it is known that the American Eskimo Dog is a modern variation of a very ancient family of dogs.

The Spitz Family

That ancient family is the spitz family, dogs possessing many wolflike characteristics: erect pointed ears, double coats, and moderation in

"I'm all yours..."

body proportions. Most of this family flourished in cold, unforgiving environments, and served humans in functions requiring courage, strength, intelligence, and determination.

In the harsh northern world, there was little patience for a dog that could not pull its weight or more. Thus there was rigorous selection for a hardy dog that could serve as a draft animal, hunter, and watchdog. These traits continue to make this family popular today. The Alaskan Malamute, Siberian Husky, Samoyed, Chow Chow, Keeshond, Pomeranian, and American Eskimo Dog are all members of this strong-willed group.

Family Pet

The American Eskimo Dog is in many ways not the prototypical spitz. While still retaining the tenacious spirit and attitude of its ancestors, the Eskie's most important role is that of family pet. It is the modern-day answer to the jack-of-all-trades dog: vocal watchdog, lively helpmate, and affectionate companion. So how did this little dog evolve?

Background

As many of the spitz breeds overspread Europe, different areas developed distinct subgroups of spitz dogs, which eventually became distinguished by their place of origin. The most well documented of these is the German Spitz, which was bred in five separate sizes, each having within it separate lines based upon color. Today's Keeshond and Pomeranian descend partly from two of these varieties. The Eskie probably descends from several varieties of the German Spitz, in addition to more recent influence from the Keeshond and the Pomeranian. In each size variety there existed pure white strains. In addition, the Italian Spitz (Volpino Italiano), a small, white dog similar to today's Eskies, was probably incorporated into the breeding pool.

With the Keeshond and Pomeranian becoming established in Britain, and then America, fanciers drafted standards to describe desired features. In part, the Eskimo Dog owes its existence to the exclusion of similar dogs from the Keeshond and Pomeranian standards. Although the Keeshond originally came in several colors, including white, when fanciers chose to accept only the gray color, the white dogs of this breed were suddenly excluded. Although the often white Pomeranian was originally recognized in two size varieties, when the larger (over 8 pounds [3.6 kg]) variety was dropped, these dogs, too, lost breed recognition. Thus, in the early part of the twentieth century there were two groups of related purebred dogs, both excluded from recognition, and both with considerable numbers. Lacking official breed status,

and without an organized breed club, the fate of these dogs has become obscured with time.

The Spitz Becomes American

Although these were far from banner years in the show ring for these small white Spitz Dogs, something more important was happening. Undaunted by the lack of such formalities as kennel club recognition, owners of these versatile dogs continued to cherish them. European emigrants to America brought with them their most-valued possessions, among them their German Spitz Dogs. The little white Spitz Dogs flourished and were quick to adopt America as their own. In fact, it was short order before they came to be commonly called the American Spitz.

Circus Dogs

The American Spitz soon found its way into Americana through another route: the circus. In the early 1920s, these dazzling daredevils were a favorite circus attraction—performing tricks to music, in acts with clowns or ponies, wire walking, and even weaving in and out of moving wagon wheel spokes and horses' hooves. One of the most striking acts was the all-white statue act, where white dogs, white horses, and white painted and costumed humans would perform different tricks, freezing in various poses at intervals so that they appeared to be one large intricate marble statue. Stout's Pal Pierre, an Eskie with Barnum and Bailey circus, was the first dog to walk a tightrope. With their dazzling white coats, obvious good humor, quick intelligence, and uncanny abilities, many early circus-going families left with a vision of a Spitz as their next dog. And in fact, there were often

The American Eskimo Dog: versatile worker, talented circus performer, and unrivaled companion.

puppies available from the circus, so that wherever the circus traveled, a small but influential trail of Spitzes and Spitz admirers remained. With the illustrious heritage of famous circus dogs, new owners were eager to record the performing dogs in their dog's backgrounds, complete with information about tricks performed and the circus with which they performed. Many Eskie pedigrees can still be traced back to these famous working circus dogs.

UKC Recognition

The registry of purebred dogs for show purposes in the United States has been dominated by the American Kennel Club (AKC). Although not invited into the auspices of AKC recognition, the American Spitz was recognized as a breed by the other principal registry, the United Kennel Club (UKC). The two kennel clubs differed fundamentally in the requirement for registering an individual dog as purebred. The AKC was then and is now primarily a pedigree-based registry; it required that a certain number of generations of a dog's ancestry be documented and recorded with some AKC-recognized registering body before according it registration. The UKC's emphasis was upon working ability, and as such put more value upon the individual dog than the dog's background. In recognition of the fact that many purebred dogs existed without documented pedigrees, they allowed individuals to be single-registered as a particular breed as long as sufficient evidence was submitted that a dog was typical for its breed. In order to encourage purity of ancestry, the UKC awards the Purple Ribbon (P.R.) title to dogs having seven generations of ancestors registered with the UKC. The allowance of single-registration was a boon to the American Spitz, because the breed enjoyed a grassroots popularity, with little emphasis upon pedigrees and show dogs.

Name Change

One last change was made to make the American Spitz a household name—and that was a name change. In the wake of World War I, with anti-German sentiment strong, the Germanic *Spitz* was replaced by the more American *Eskimo*, so the breed became known as the American Eskimo. It's said the name came from the kennel name of the first of these dogs to be registered with the UKC back in 1913.

The Eskie is a do-it-all kind of dog.

Dog of the People

The combination of the circus performers and word of mouth continued to make the American Eskimo Dog a "dog of the people." Most new Eskie owners did not choose their breed from a book, but fell in love with their neighbor's wonderful white dog and had to have one just like it. Dogs were single-registered with UKC, but only a handful of diligent breeders methodically registered all of their stock.

Standard

For many years there was no breed standard, no breed club, and no breed shows, so that registration entitled owners to limited opportunities compared to other breeds. Although a prototypical breed standard was advanced in the late 1950s, it was not until 1970 that the standard

was officially adopted, the first show for Eskies was held, and the National American Eskimo Dog Association (NAEDA) was founded. At that time NAEDA made an important decision that would forever change the Eskie's place in dogdom: the UKC would no longer accept single-registrations for Eskies. They realized that the effect of the single-registration policy was to promote a suspicion among the public that the American Eskimo was not purebred. As long as single-registration was allowed, there was the possibility that a dog could be registered as an Eskie that happened to be a lucky mix. And as long as this was a possibility, the American Eskimo could never hope to gain recognition from kennel clubs that based registration on pedigree documentation.

Because of this decision, the Eskie finally gained the respect from the dog world that it so richly deserved. Now Champion and Grand Champion Eskies grace Purple Ribbon pedigrees. In fact, because single-registration has been closed since 1970, enough generations have passed so that almost all present-day Eskies carry the P.R. title as a matter of course.

AKC Recognition

But even though single-registration no longer stood in the way of AKC recognition, the AKC requirement of submitting the breed's UKC studbook for inspection could not be complied with by the UKC. Instead, another national breed club was formed, the American Eskimo Dog Club of America (AEDCA) to register Eskies and collect pedigree information for submission to the AKC. Between its inception in 1985 and submission of its records to the AKC in 1993, over 1,750 Eskies were registered with AEDCA. These dogs, along with a few more allowed in an eight-month grace period, form the gene pool for the AKC American Eskimo.

Note: One more name change had been made: from American Eskimo to American Eskimo Dog.

In January 1994, the first American Eskimo Dog stepped foot into an AKC ring. Like all new breeds, it debuted in the Miscellaneous Class. It was in that class only briefly. In July 1995, the American Eskimo Dog was accepted as a regular AKC breed. It is classified in the Non-Sporting group, that eclectic group of dogs that have as their main function that of companion.

New Registrations

Because only a small percentage of the UKC Eskies were registered with the AKC, the AKC gave owners a second chance to bring more foundation dogs into the AKC gene pool. Between May of 2000 and May of 2003, the books were opened to new registrations. Although the AKC-registered Eskies still represent only a small percentage of the UKC-registered ones, they tend to be those from serious breeders and exhibitors, ensuring that the AKC foundation was made up of the best Eskies available. Most of the AKC Eskies are also dual registered with the UKC.

One Size Does Not Fit All

One happy result of the Eskie's varied origins is the diversity of sizes present in the breed today. The UKC recognizes two varieties: the standard and the miniature, whereas the AKC

recognizes three varieties: standard (over 15 to 19 inches [38.1–45.3 cm]), miniature (over 12 to 15 inches [30.5–38.1 cm]), and toy (9 to 12 inches [22.9–30.5 cm]). The bonus of having several sizes from which to choose makes it even easier for prospective owners to find the right dog that suits their lifestyles.

At first glance the Eskie appears to be a miniature version of the Samoyed, but closer inspection reveals that the two are not proportioned the same. The Eskie has smaller bones, and tends to be slightly longer in body than the Samoyed. Nor is the Eskie a larger version of the Pomeranian, again having comparatively smaller bones and a longer body, with not necessarily so profuse a coat.

The Eskie's Future

The American Eskimo Dog—a breed both ancient and modern, both ignored and applauded—now faces a new challenge. With its natural flash it is a favorite at dog shows; but with such popularity comes the danger that the breed will be changed into a caricature of itself. So far, breeders are preserving the breed's qualities—after all, why mess with a good thing?

ESKIE ESSENTIALS

Most people are initially attracted to a breed because of its looks, and the stunning white Eskie is no exception.

Far too often dogs are acquired with the idea that all breeds act the same. They don't. The very reason that different breeds were initially created stemmed from differences in behavior, not looks. Dogs were selected for their propensity to trail, point, retrieve, herd, protect, or even cuddle, with physical attributes often secondary to behavioral.

Temperament

So what is in an Eskie's genes?

✔ There are individual differences, but the typical Eskie is an alert, bright, quick-witted dog, wonderfully obedient but sometimes playfully mischievous.

✔ The Eskie is loving, demonstrative without being fawning, and is extremely loyal to its family.

✔ The Eskie thinks of itself as a family member, and expects to be treated like one. Do not

The typical Eskie has the potential to be a wonderful companion for the right owner.

expect an Eskie to be happy if banished to the yard.

✔ The Eskie is an excellent watchdog, but does not have the physical attributes to be an intimidating protection dog. Sometimes barking can become excessive.

✔ Although not one-person dogs, Eskies do take a while to warm up to strangers. They *must* be well socialized as youngsters, or this natural wariness can be expressed as shyness and even fear biting.

✔ Although Eskies may occasionally be headstrong, in general they are a "soft" breed and tend to be extremely sensitive to harsh words or corrections.

Problem Behaviors

In a survey of Eskimo Dog owners, barking and digging were listed as the most common problem behaviors, followed by shyness and hyperactivity. Biting, destructive behavior, escaping, and dog fighting were rarely a problem with properly socialized Eskies. Some poorly bred Eskies can have nasty temperaments, so you should select your particular Eskie with great care.

Grooming

Keeping the Eskie's coat gleaming, full, and white is not as daunting a task as it might first appear. Its coat texture is such that dirt does not cling, and even mud will fall from the coat as it dries (of course, this may be in your house!). This texture, coupled with a relative lack of oiliness, also tends to be resistant to easy matting, and best of all, the Eskie is virtually free of doggy odor! It is also a good breed for allergic dog owners, as the Eskie sheds minimal dog dander.

Eskies enjoy being groomed, and they should be brushed at least once or twice a week. Males will shed profusely once a year, unspayed females twice a year. During shedding periods

Eskie Rating

Energy level:	●●●
Playfulness:	●●●●
Exercise needs:	●●●
Affection level:	●●●
Friendliness toward dogs:	●●
Friendliness toward other pets:	●●
Friendliness toward strangers:	●●
Ease of training:	●●●●
Watchdog ability:	●●●●
Protection ability:	●
Grooming requirements:	●●●
Cold tolerance:	●●●●
Heat tolerance:	●

Key: ●●●● = Very high
●●● = High
●● = Average
● = Below average

they should be groomed more frequently; still, be prepared for your home to be "frosted" with a fine coating of white hair during shedding season.

Health

Eskies typically live 12 to 14 years, and do so with minimal health problems. Progressive retinal atropy (PRA), patellar luxation, and hip dysplasia, which are detailed on pages 70 to 74, occur in the breed. A DNA test is available for PRA, and the Orthopedic Foundation for Animals offers certification for normal hips and patellas.

Finding the Right American Eskimo Dog for You

Now that you have decided that an American Eskimo Dog is indeed the dog for you, congratulations—but don't stop now! You'll want to just as carefully locate the right individual for you. And there are a lot of choices to be made.

Standard, Miniature, or Toy?

After seeing several Eskies, you probably have already formed an opinion about which size most appeals to you. But if undecided, consider that the larger dog will need more room to exercise, take up more room in the car (and maybe bed!), shed more, and eat more; however, if you want a jogging companion or slightly more intimidating watchdog, the standard should be your choice. The smaller sizes are more vulnerable to attacks from other dogs and injuries from rough children, but may fare better in apartments or as lapdogs. Some of the smaller sizes may be more vocal and active, and also may not be as good with children. True toy Eskies are hard to come by, and will probably be more expensive to purchase.

Finally, remember that if you are buying a puppy, breeders can only give you an estimate, not a guarantee, of what size they expect the puppy to be as an adult. This is especially true when the pedigree contains dogs of many different sizes. A pedigree of standard-sized Eskies will fairly reliably produce standards; a pedigree of miniature-sized Eskies will fairly reliably produce miniatures. The toys tend to be a little less reliable, with some from toy backgrounds still growing larger. Pedigrees with dogs of many sizes are apt to produce dogs of many sizes.

Puppy or Adult?

Although most prospective owners think in terms of getting a puppy, don't dismiss the idea of acquiring an older Eskie. No one can deny that a puppy is cute and fun, but a puppy is much like a baby; you can't ever be too busy to walk, feed, supervise, or clean. If you work or have limited patience, consider an older puppy or adult that won't require so much intensive care. One advantage of the Eskie's personality is that it is not a "one-person dog" so it can form new bonds fairly easily. On the other hand, an adult may arrive with a host of bad habits; if raised in a kennel, an older dog may have a difficult time adjusting to family life or children.

Most puppies are ideally brought home between 8 and 12 weeks of age, but if you definitely want a show-quality dog you may have to wait until the pups are much older. No matter what the age, if the puppy has been properly socialized, your Eskie will soon blend into your family life and love you as though it's always owned you.

TIP

Sizing up the Eskie
✔ Toy:　　　　Height: 9–12 inches
　　　　　　　　(23–30 cm)
　　　　　　　Weight: 6–10 pounds
　　　　　　　　(2.7–4.5 kg)
✔ Miniature:　Height: 12–15 inches
　　　　　　　　(30–38 cm)
　　　　　　　Weight: 11–20 pounds
　　　　　　　　(4.98–9 kg)
✔ Standard:　Height: 15–19 inches
　　　　　　　　(38–48 cm)
　　　　　　　Weight: 20–40 pounds
　　　　　　　　(9.1–18 kg)

Male or Female?

The choice of male versus female is largely one of personal preference, but keep the following pros and cons in mind.

Male Eskies are slightly larger and carry a more profuse coat. They enjoy strutting around and showing off, especially if there is a cute Eskie girl around. Unless neutered, they tend to become preoccupied with sniffing and marking when on walks, and some may also lift their legs in the house. They can also roam in search of female friends, and if they are around one in heat, they are inconsolable. Intact (unneutered) Eskie males do not take well to other intact males, and may fight.

Female Eskies are more delicate in appearance. After each season (or heat), they will shed profusely and lose a good deal of their coats. These seasons occur about twice a year and last for three weeks, during which time you must

keep your Eskie away from amorous neighbor-hood males who have chosen your house as the place to be. You must also contend with her bloody discharge during her season, either by exiling her from your white carpets (remember the ones you got so her hair wouldn't show up?) or by fitting her with those cute little panties (which she will inevitably be wearing when the person you most want to impress arrives at your home unexpectedly).

Most of the problems associated with either sex can be overcome by neutering. And if the prospects of making more money by breeding an Eskie of one sex as opposed to the other enter into your decision, you should reconsider getting an Eskie at all. You're adding a family member, not livestock; besides, if you depend on the money you could make from breeding Eskies, expect to become very poor!

Pet, Show, or Breeding Quality?

Although at first glance all Eskies resemble one another, to the experienced eye there are dramatic differences between individuals. The standard of perfection for the breed does not cover every detail and is open to interpretation in several areas. In addition, some breeders may emphasize flawless movement in their stock, whereas others will sacrifice perfect movement for exquisite facial expression, and still others insist upon a profuse ice white coat. As you see more Eskies from different kennels, these differ-ences will become more apparent to you, and you may begin to form an opinion as to which traits are most important to you. The more sub-tle differences will probably matter to you only if you wish to acquire a show- or breeding-quality dog. No matter what, the traits that you should never compromise are good tempera-ment and good health. Even a show dog must first and foremost be a pet.

Pet-quality dogs: Although no dog is perfect, pet-quality dogs have one or more traits that would make winning with them in the show ring difficult. A common reason in males is the failure of one or both testicles to descend into the scrotum. Such dogs can be gorgeous breed representatives, but cannot be shown. However, most veterinarians suggest the retained testicle be removed as it is more cancer-prone, so this is an added expense you must anticipate. Another reason might be any of several small flaws that would never be evident to any but the most ardent Eskie fancier—flaws such as a missing tooth, a long back, or straight shoulders. These, too, make beautiful pets.

Somewhat questionable are those with flaws that make them non-Eskie-like (remember, you want an Eskie in part because you like how they look, right?). Such a flaw might be a blue eye, a pink nose, or a very short tail.

Finally, there are flaws that make pet quality not even pet quality: flaws in temperament such as shyness or aggressiveness.

Show-quality dogs: Show-quality dogs should be able to compete in the show ring with a reasonable expectation of finishing a championship. Showing a dog can open an entire new world of exciting wins, crushing losses, eccentric friends, travel to exotic fairgrounds in remote cities, and endless opportunities to spend money. It is inexplicably addicting. You should attend several shows before deciding you want to be a participant. Your search for a show-quality dog will require considerable effort on your part. A show-quality Eskie should be AKC-registered, not just UKC, because the AKC holds many more dog shows.

Begin by seeing as many Eskies in real life (at dog shows or breeders' homes) and in print (books and magazines) as possible. Ask breeders what they consider to be the good and bad points of their stock. Be forewarned: it will be a rare day when two breeders agree on what is the most perfect Eskie, so in the end it will be up to you alone to make an informed choice based upon your own sense of Eskie esthetics.

In Search of Eskie Excellence

Even if you are not looking for a world-beater show dog, you still want to be very careful about where you find your Eskimo Dog. Common sources follow:

Dog Magazines

A quick way to contact several serious breeders is to look in the classified section of one of the monthly dog magazines (such as *Dog World*) available at larger newsstands. The disadvantage is that if the breeder is located a distance from you, you will not be able to evaluate his dogs in the flesh, and you will not be able to choose your own puppy. Also, shipping adds an additional expense and can be stressful for an older puppy.

Dog Shows

You can contact the UKC or AKC for the date of a show in your area; these are also listed in *Dog World* magazine. Most shows start at 9 A.M., so unless you know when the Eskies are being judged you must get there early or risk missing them altogether. Tell the Eskie exhibitors of your interest and arrange to talk with several after they have finished in the show ring. Incidentally, don't be swayed by who wins or loses on that one day. It's *your* opinion that matters, not that of one judge.

Why contact show breeders if all you want is a pet? Because these breeders will have raised your pet as though it were their next Best in Show winner. It will have received the same prenatal care, nutrition, and socialization as every prospective show dog in that litter. And these breeders should be knowledgeable and conscientious enough to have also considered temperament and health when planning the breeding. They should have the results of DNA tests for PRA, and OFA evaluations for both parents.

Most show breeders will demand you stay in touch throughout your dog's life; in fact, you may find yourself part of a very large extended family. Not only does this mean that advice is just a phone call away, but also friendship and help when it's needed. Finally, because in some sense the non-show puppy is a by-product of the litter, these breeders are not out to make a buck from these puppies, and prices are generally quite reasonable.

Look for responsible breeders exhibiting at dog shows, especially American Eskimo Dog specialty shows. The UKC and AKC American Eskimo Dog clubs can give you a list of breeders in your area.

✔ Join one of the many Eskie Internet discussion groups (you can find several through *www. yahoogroups.com*) and let breeders know something about you and what you're looking for.

✔ Search the Internet for breeder Web sites. Avoid those that seem willing to sell mail-order puppies without first getting to know you.

✔ Look for clues that you are dealing with a responsible breeder.

Responsible breeders:

• Breed only one or two breeds of dogs, so they can concentrate on just those breeds.

• Breed no more than three or four litters per year, so they can concentrate on those litters.

• Can compare their dogs objectively to the American Eskimo Dog standard.

• Can discuss Eskie health concerns and provide evidence of the health of their own dogs.

• Can give substantial reasons relating to quality of conformation, temperament, and health, why they bred the litter, or chose those parents.

• Have pictures of several generations of the puppy's ancestors.

• Have clean, outgoing adults.

• Have clean facilities that promote interaction with their dogs.

• Raise their litter inside the house and underfoot, not in a kennel or garage.

• Question you about your facilities, your prior experiences with dogs, and your intentions regarding your new dog.

• Sell companion-quality puppies with only AKC limited registration, which means their progeny cannot be registered, or with spay-neuter agreements.

• Insist upon taking the dog back should you be unable to keep it at any time during its life.

Reskies

There comes a time when all your plans to buy only the best-bred Eskie fall by the wayside. That time is when you meet an Eskie in need. Eskies end up in rescue for many reasons. Perhaps they were lost and never claimed, perhaps their owners died, or perhaps their owners simply tired of having a dog. Those with responsible breeders often find a safe haven back with their breeders, but too many have no place to turn. They are filled with love but have no family to share it with. Occasionally they have behavior problems, often stemming from poor training or socialization, but good rescue organizations will make sure you know any problems ahead of time and will help you guide your Eskie to becoming the best dog he can be. Rescue Eskies, or Reskies, range from puppies to seniors, but have in common a need for a forever home they can call their own. Check out page 92 for a list of American Eskimo Dog rescue groups.

Contacting the Breeder

If you have decided to contact a breeder, you should prepare a list of questions so that you can narrow the field further. Tell the breeder how you heard of him or her and exactly what you want. It is not fair to you or the breeder to ask for a show puppy you never intend to show, and it is equally unfair to both of you to get a pet puppy and then try to show it. Many, many hard feelings have arisen because of this seemingly small oversight. Expect the breeder to ask you something about yourself, your facilities, and your experience with dogs or Eskies in particular.

Note: If you really want a show prospect, you will probably have to demonstrate to the breeder that you are serious. You do this by learning as much as possible about American Eskimo Dogs and their care before calling, but by also admitting that you don't know it all and are eager to learn.

1. How often are litters available? If new litters are always in the works, you might worry that the breeder is aiming for profit, not quality.

2. Ask about the parents. Do they have conformation or obedience titles? This is not only important if you want a show/obedience prospect, but again can give you a clue about the care taken with the litter.

3. What kind of temperaments do the parents and the puppies have?

4. If some puppies are being sold as pet-quality, why?

5. What health clearances do the parents have? What guarantees are offered?

Terms of sale: Although you're anxious to see the puppies, now is the time to ask the breeder about the terms of sale. Don't fall in love with a puppy and then have to walk away because an agreement could not be reached. There are several possibilities, the easiest being that you will pay a set amount (usually cash) and receive full ownership. If registration papers cost extra, walk away. Puppy and papers should always be a package deal. If pet quality, sometimes breeders will insist upon having the puppy neutered before supplying the papers, or they may stipulate that the puppy is to have a "Limited Registration," which means it cannot be shown or bred.

Evaluating Eskie Puppies

Once you have narrowed down your list, if possible arrange to visit the breeder. If you are considering more than one breeder, be honest about it. Always go to view the puppies prepared to leave without one if you don't see exactly what you want. Remember, no good breeder wants you to take a puppy you are not 110 percent crazy about. Don't lead the breeder on if you have decided against a purchase; he or she may have another buyer in line. Finally, don't bounce from one breeder to another on the same day, and certainly do not visit the animal shelter beforehand. Puppies are vulnerable to many deadly diseases that you can transmit by way of your hands, clothes, and shoes. How tragic it would be if the breeder's invitation for you to view his or her babies ended up killing them.

American Eskimo Dog Registration

The breeder should have contacted either the AKC or UKC upon birth of the litter, and received a litter packet containing registration applications for each puppy. You should not leave with your puppy without the registration application signed by both you and the breeder. This is an extremely valuable document; do not misplace it or forget to send it in! Ask the breeder if there are any requirements concerning the puppy's registered name; most show breeders will want the first name to be their kennel name. You should also have received a pedigree with your puppy; if not, you can buy a copy of its pedigree from the AKC or UKC when you send in the registration papers.

CHECKLIST

Handling and Holding the Puppy

1 These babies are fragile little beings, and you must be extremely careful where you step and how you handle them.

2 If you have children with you, don't allow them to run around or play with the puppies unsupervised.

3 In addition, your entire family should know how to properly handle a puppy.

4 Never pick up a puppy by its legs or head or tail.

5 Cradle the puppy with both hands, one under the chest, the other under the hindquarters, and with the side of the pup secure against your chest.

Most modern "kennels" are a collection of only a few dogs that are first of all the breeder's pets themselves.

✔ However large or small the operation, look for facilities that are clean and safe. Again, these are clues about the care given your prospective puppy.

✔ Does the breeder treat the dogs with love and respect? Even at a young age, mistreatment might have damaged your puppy's temperament.

✔ The adults should be clean, groomed, and in apparent good health. They should neither try to attack you nor cower from you. Look to the adults for the dog your puppy will become. If you don't care for their looks or temperaments, say good-bye.

✔ The dam will not look her best, so ask to see pictures of her (and the sire) in full bloom. If no such pictures are available, then proceed with caution.

Finally, the puppies! As you look upon this undulating snowstorm of Eskie-ettes, how will you ever decide? If you want a show puppy, let the breeder decide. In fact, the breeder knows the puppies' personalities better than you will in the short time you can evaluate them, so listen carefully to any suggestions the breeder has even for a pet. But first decide if this is the litter for you:

✔ By eight weeks of age, baby Eskies should look like miniature adults. Of course, they won't have the coat development, or coordination, and their ears may not yet be erect, but they should generally be recognizable as American Eskimo Dogs. Dark nose pigmentation, absent at birth, should be present by this age.

✔ Normal Eskie puppies are friendly, curious, and attentive. If they are apathetic or sleeping, it could be because they have just eaten, but it could also be because they are sickly.

✔ The puppies should be clean, with no missing hair, crusted or reddened skin, or signs of parasites.

✔ Eyes, ears, and nose should be free of discharge (although a slight watery discharge from the eyes is not uncommon in Eskies). Examine the eyelids if such a discharge is present to ensure that it is not due to the lids or lashes rolling in on the eye and causing irritation.

✔ The teeth should be straight and meet up evenly, with the top incisors just overlapping the lower incisors.

✔ The gums should be pink; pale gums may indicate anemia.

✔ The area around the anus should have no hint of irritation or recent diarrhea.

Few breeds give you such a choice of size!

✔ Puppies should not be thin or excessively potbellied.
✔ By the age of 12 weeks, male puppies should have both testicles descended in the scrotum.

If the puppy of your choice is limping, or exhibits any of the above traits, express your concern and ask to either come back next week to see if it has improved, or to have your veterinarian examine it. In fact, any puppy you select should be purchased with the stipulation that it is pending an immediate health check (at your expense) by your veterinarian. The breeder should furnish you with a complete medical history including dates of vaccinations and worming.

You may still find it nearly impossible to decide which bouncing puffball will be yours. Don't worry: no matter which one you choose, it will be the best one. In years to come, you will wonder how you were so lucky to have picked the wonder Eskie of the century—you must realize that your Eskie will be wonderful in part because you are going to make it so!

and finally the proud but frail senior. Be sure that you remember the promise you made to yourself and your future puppy before you made the commitment to share your life: to keep your interest in your dog and care for him every day of his life with as much love and enthusiasm as you did the first day he arrived home. Your life may change dramatically in the years to come: divorce, new baby, new home—for better or worse, your Eskie will still depend on you and still love you, and you need to remain as loyal to your Eskie as your Eskie will be to you.

A Lifetime Shared

You have a lifetime of experiences to share with your new Eskie. The remainder of your dog's life will be spent under your care and guidance. Both of you will change through the years. Accept that your Eskie will change as he matures—from the cute, eager-to-please baby, to the cute, mischievous, often disobedient adolescent, then to the self-reliant adult partner,

Whether show-quality or pet-quality,
all Eskies are fun-quality!

YOUR ESKIMO PUPPY

Every puppy needs the undivided attention of its new family at this crucial time in its life.

Once you've chosen your special puppy, you probably can't wait to bring her home. But hold on—it's not fair to either of you to bring a new baby into the house unless you have made all of the necessary preparations beforehand. So channel your excitement, get the entire family involved, and make sure everything is just perfect for the new addition.

An Eskie Shopping Spree

If you are a bona fide shopping enthusiast, here's your big chance. Having a new dog will provide you with an excuse to go on a wild shopping spree for all sorts of Eskie essentials. A visit to a large pet shop, a dog show vendor aisle, or a glance through one of the pet supply mail-order catalogs or Web sites will regale you with items you never imagined a dog could need. But even if shopping is not your idea of fun, there are a few essentials you must have:

Good luck choosing!

Collars: First, your Eskie will need a collar, two collars, in fact. A round nylon buckle collar is best for around the house. A slip (choke) collar is actually safer for walking in public, because a scared puppy can pull backward out of a buckle collar. However, a slip collar is far too dangerous to ever leave on your Eskie unattended. An identification tag should be affixed to the buckle collar. Harnesses also work well for Eskies.

Leash: A nylon, web, or leather leash is another necessity. Chain leashes are difficult to handle and tend to smack the puppy in the face, so should be avoided. The retractable leashes are very handy for walking an older puppy, but be careful not to drop these leashes. When dropped, the handle retracts quickly toward the dog and some puppies think it is chasing them, causing them to run from it in fright!

Food and water bowls: You will need flat-bottomed food and water bowls. Eskie puppies love to play in water, so be sure the water bowl is not easily tipped. Stainless steel bowls are gen-

The Christmas Puppy

The Christmas puppy is practically an American tradition—such a heartwarming scene is portrayed by the children discovering the baby asleep among the other gifts beneath the tree on Christmas morning. But this is a fantasy scene. The real scene is more often that of a crying, confused baby that may have vented its anxiety on the other gifts and left you some additional "gifts" of its own beneath the tree!

Don't bring a new puppy into the hectic chaos of Christmas morning. Not only does this add to what is bound to be a very confusing and intimidating transition for your Eskie, but a puppy should not be expected to compete with all of the toys and games that children may be receiving. Instead, a photograph or videotape of your special Eskie-to-be (perhaps along with some Eskie paraphernalia) will have to suffice until some of the holiday madness has subsided. Meanwhile, the whole family can get involved in preparing for baby.

erally best; some dogs can have an allergic reaction to plastic. Be sure to find out what your puppy is eating and try to feed the same food.

Bed: No doubt you have your own bed where you sleep at night. Where will your puppy's bed be? Your Eskie will appreciate having her own bed readily available whenever sleep overtakes her. A crate large enough so that your Eskie can stand and turn around when full grown provides an ideal bed. The crate will also be an invaluable house-training tool, and a means of keeping your puppy out of trouble when you can't be there to watch. Think of it as you would a baby's crib: a place for peace and protection. And just as with a child, the crib or crate is a place for bedtime and naptime, but not a place of exile or a place to spend entire days. Plastic crates are readily available, economical, and approved for airline shipping. Wire crates allow more ventilation and visibility, and fold for easy storage and transport. Place an easily washed towel or blanket in the crate: Eskies appreciate a soft bed!

Exercise pen: You may find an exercise pen (commonly referred to as an "X-Pen") to be a helpful purchase. These are transportable wire folding "playpens" for dogs, typically about 4×4 feet (1.2×1.2 m). This makes a handy indoor enclosure when you can't be watching.

Baby gates: Baby gates are also a big help; puppies do not protest as much when blocked by a baby gate as when blocked by a closed door, plus you can keep an eye on them.

Anti-chew preparations: Some of the anti-chew preparations may help protect your furniture and walls, but do not rely exclusively on them. Toys, chewbones, and a keen eye are the best furniture protectors.

Grooming tools: Although your young Eskie won't require much grooming, you will still need a soft brush and some nail clippers. The items an adult Eskie needs are described in the grooming section, beginning on page 57.

First-aid kit: You should also get your first-aid kit together, as described in the veterinary section, page 68.

Toys: Your Eskie puppy will want some toys she can call her own. Rawhide bones are excellent for satisfying the urge to chew. A ball, of course, is a necessity! Many Eskies will take very good care of stuffed animals, and seem to espe-

Eskies may love playing in the great outdoors, but they are not dogs that should live outside.

cially enjoy them as toys (make sure the eyes and nose will not come off; also, avoid those stuffed with Styrofoam beads or straw unless you really enjoy vacuuming). Sturdy squeaky toys are also enjoyable (for them, but not always for their owners!); make sure the squeaker is secure. Homemade toys of plastic milk cartons are also big favorites. Never give toys that are so small they could be inhaled and lodge in the windpipe. But don't be tempted to use an old shoe—when the puppy happens upon your closet full of new shoes, she may think she's arrived at the toy store and start chewing!

Eskie Quarters

Decide now where you intend to keep your new family member. If you intend to have an exclusively outdoor dog, stop right now and please reconsider your choice of an American Eskimo Dog. This breed is not amenable to being kept separated from its family. Although its thick coat enables the Eskie to enjoy cold weather (within reason), hot weather can be intolerable. So plan for your Eskie to spend at least part of its time in the house with the rest of your family.

Indoors: It is best that the new puppy not have the run of the entire house. Choose an easily Eskie-proofed room where you spend a lot of time, preferably one that is close to a door leading outside. Kitchens and dens are usually ideal. When you must leave your dog for some time, you may wish to place her in a crate, secure room, or outdoor kennel. Garages have the disadvantage of also housing many toxic items; bathrooms have the disadvantage of being so confining and isolated that puppies may become destructive.

Doghouse: If you keep your Eskie outside while you are gone you must provide shelter, preferably a cozy doghouse. The ideal doghouse has a removable top for easy cleaning, and a windbreak so that the door does not lead directly into sleeping quarters. You may wish to place the house within a small absolutely secure kennel for your peace of mind. Some people combine a kennel run with a doggy door leading to an enclosure in a garage, or to a separate room in the house.

Baby Steps

It's time! If possible, arrange to take a few days off of work so that you can spend time with your new family member. At the very least, bring the puppy home on a weekend so that the first day with you won't be one spent alone.

Pitchforks and puppies—a bad combination. Start puppy-proofing now!

The Ride Home

The ride home with you may be the puppy's first time in a car, and her first time away from the security of her home and former family. Bring plenty of towels in case she gets carsick. If possible, bring a family member to hold and comfort the puppy on the ride home. If it is a long ride, bring a crate. Never let a new puppy roam around the car, where she can cause, and have, accidents. Spend some time at the breeder's house while the puppy gets acquainted with you, and listen carefully to the breeder's instructions. Arrange for the puppy not to have eaten before leaving with you; this reduces the possibility of car sickness and helps the puppy learn that you will be her new provider when you get to her new home.

The Name

Incidentally, be sure to ask the breeder what name your puppy knows. Most breeders call all of their puppies by some generic name, such as "Pup." Just continue to call yours by the same name until you have something better picked out. Your puppy will learn a new name quickly at this age, especially if it means food or fun. Be careful about the name you choose; for example, the ever popular Eskie name "Snowball" unfortunately sounds a lot like "No Ball" and is a confusing choice for a name. Test your chosen name to be sure that it does not sound like a reprimand or command.

Bathroom Area

When you get home, put the puppy on-lead and carry it to the spot you have decided will be the bathroom. Once the puppy relieves herself, let her explore a little and then offer her a small meal.

Once the puppy has eaten, she will probably have to relieve herself again, so take her back out to the part of the yard you have designated as the bathroom. Remember to praise enthusiastically when she eliminates in the right place.

Time for Bed

When your Eskie begins to act sleepy, place her in her crate so that she knows this is her special bed. A stuffed toy, hot water bottle, or ticking clock may help alleviate some of the anxiety of being left alone. You may wish to place the crate in your bedroom for this first night so that the puppy may be comforted by your presence. Remember, this is the scariest thing that has ever happened in your puppy's short life; she has been uprooted from the security of a mother, littermates, and loving breeder, so you must be comforting and reassuring on this crucial first night.

Off-limits Training

You should have decided before your puppy came home what parts of your home will be off-limits. Make sure that every family member understands the rules, and that they understand that sneaking the puppy onto off-limit furniture, for example, is not doing the puppy any favor at all. Your puppy will naturally want to explore everywhere you let her, including climbing on furniture. When she does, take her to her own bed, or get down on the floor with her.

The use of mousetraps on furniture, as advocated by some, is potentially dangerous and not advisable. There are several more humane items (available through pet catalogs) that emit a loud tone when a dog jumps on furniture, but these should not be necessary if you train your young puppy gently and consistently from the beginning.

TIP

Visitors, Play, and Pets

Now is not the time for all the neighbors to come visiting. You want your puppy to know who her new family members will be, and more people will only add to the youngster's confusion. Nor is it the time for rough and tumble play, which could scare the puppy. Introductions to other family pets might also be better postponed.

House-training Your Eskie

The sooner you start house-training, the better. Not just because you don't want to ruin your carpets, but because to a puppy, urinating and defecating are self-rewarding behaviors. Emptying a full bladder or bowel feels good, so wherever your Eskie puppy happens to relieve herself, she will be rewarded by that feeling—and dogs repeat behaviors that are rewarded. Your job is to make sure she gets rewarded for pottying outside, and not rewarded for pottying inside.

The longer you put off house-training, the more rewarding experiences your puppy has pottying indoors. Simply pushing her out the door won't be good enough to overcome the convenience of the indoors. You have to make it more rewarding to go outside. You must go outside with her, no matter how busy you are or how bad the weather is; otherwise, she will just huddle by the door waiting for you to let her back in and then potty on your floor. Take some treats out with you, wait until your dog has pottied, and then instantly praise and reward her for doing it outside.

Restricting Your Puppy

Your Eskie may have learned it's rewarding to go outside, but if she already was pottying inside, you'll have some remedial work to do. Puppies naturally avoid soiling their denning area, but they don't go far in the effort. The solution is to restrict your puppy to a dog den-sized area, such as a dog crate, anytime you can't supervise her and there's a chance of her relieving herself. This teaches your puppy the beginnings of self-control, and reduces the chances of her rewarding herself by pottying inside.

Your puppy can't live in a crate; she needs plenty of outside time to play and socialize. But as she gets better at holding herself, you can gradually enlarge the designated den area.

✔ Place her bed or crate in a tiny enclosed area—an area only a couple of feet beyond the boundary of her bed.

✔ Do everything you can to prevent her from soiling this area, taking her outside often. You are forming a habit: in the den, no potty; out of the den, potty.

✔ Once she goes several days without soiling her den, make it just a little bit larger. You can have her den area in the kitchen or family room so she's able to socialize with the rest of the family without having unlimited freedom.

✔ As her house-training progresses you will be gradually expanding her den so that eventually she'll have access to an entire room, then another, and another.

Signs: Watch closely for signs of impending potty. Immediately after your puppy awakens, within 15 minutes after eating, or anytime during intense play, she will have to go potty. If she exercises a lot she'll drink a lot more water, and a while later she'll also have to urinate. When you see her sniffing and circling, she's going to go. Get her outside as fast as possible, even if you must carry her there. When in doubt, take her out.

Doggy door: One of the best house-training tools is a doggy door. Young puppies catch on to the concept of doggy doors very quickly. You can erect a small fenced potty area outside the doggy door, and a smaller area just inside. The smaller you can make the indoor area, the more like your puppy's den it will be. If possible, fill most of the area with your puppy's crate, removing the door or propping it open securely. Now when you're gone your puppy will more likely go outside to potty, practically teaching herself!

Accidents: Accidents will happen. If you catch her in the act, give a startling *"No!"* and scoop her up and scuttle her outside as quickly as possible. If you don't catch her in the act, there's really nothing you can do. She won't understand what the problem is no matter what you do. Watch more closely next time.

Cleaning: A place that smells like urine or feces is a place that screams "Restroom!" to your dog. To clean accidents on carpeting, soak up as much liquid as possible, then apply an enzyme digester-type odor neutralizer specifically made for dog accidents. Cover the area with plastic so it doesn't dry out before the digester can break down the urine. Finally, add a nice odor, such as a mixture of lavender oil or vanilla with baking soda, to the area. Avoid ammonia-based cleaners, which can act as a welcome sign to dogs.

Most people with a new puppy have unrealistic ideas about how fast house-training takes. It's not at all uncommon for dogs of any breed to take six months or longer to learn to be even fairly house-trained.

If defecating is more a problem than urinating, be sure you're feeding higher-quality foods, which produce less stool than high fiber foods. If you feed her on schedule, she'll defecate on schedule. Of course, diarrhea negates any scheduling, and no dog can be expected to hold diarrhea in. To avoid diarrhea, avoid fatty treats and sudden diet changes. If you need to change foods, introduce new foods gradually.

Eskie Pediatrics

What will you feed your new puppy? What shots does she need? Your veterinarian is your best source of individualized health care, but you should be aware of the basics.

Baby Food

Most Eskie puppies are eager eaters. Now is the time to lay a good foundation with high-quality puppy food.

Make using the outdoor potty easy to do and worth the effort!

✔ Feed a young puppy four times a day, letting her eat as much as she wants in about 15 minutes. Then pick up the bowl.

✔ From about four to six months of age, feed her three times a day.

✔ From six to nine months of age, you can gradually cut down to twice a day.

✔ You can add snacks, but don't let her get fat. If you see her packing on the baby fat, cut down on the amount she eats per meal.

Vaccinations

Vaccinations are a necessity, but that doesn't mean the more the better. Today, veterinarians have adopted a more individualized approach to vaccination. The basic concepts of puppy vaccination remain the same, however. Without well-

Your puppy depends on you for protection from predators, parasites, and disease.

timed vaccinations your Eskie can be vulnerable to deadly communicable diseases.

Your puppy received her early immunity through her dam's colostrum during the first few days of nursing. That immunity protects her during her first few weeks of life, but it also interferes with the effectiveness of any vaccinations she receives. After several weeks the maternal immunity diminishes, making the puppy more vulnerable to disease but making vaccinations more effective. Immunity wears off at different times in different dogs, so, at around six weeks of age, a series of vaccinations are given to catch the time when they will be effective while leaving as little unprotected time as possible. During this time it's best not to take your puppy to places where unvaccinated dogs may congregate. Some deadly viruses can remain in the soil for six months after an

infected dog has shed them there.

Vaccine types: Vaccinations are divided into core vaccines, which are advisable for all dogs, and non-core vaccines, which are advisable only for some dogs. Core vaccines are those for rabies, distemper, parvovirus, and hepatitis; non-core vaccines include those for leptospirosis, corona virus, tracheobronchitis, Lyme disease, and giardia. Your veterinarian can advise you if your dog's lifestyle and environment put her at risk for these diseases.

Protocol: A sample core vaccination protocol for puppies suggests giving a three-injection series at least two weeks apart, with each injection containing distemper (or measles for the first injection), parvovirus, adenovirus 2 (CAV-2), and parainfluenza (CPIV). The series should not end before 12 weeks of age. A booster is given one year later, and then boosters are given every three years. Rabies shots should be given at 16 weeks of age, with boosters at one- to three-year intervals according to local law.

Note: Some proponents of natural rearing condemn vaccinations and refuse to use them. They use homeopathic nosodes instead, and point to the fact that their dogs don't get sick as proof that they work. However, their good fortune is probably the result of herd immunity; that is, as long as most other dogs are vaccinated they probably never come in contact with the infectious agents. No controlled study has ever supported the effectiveness of nosodes. Vaccinations are not without a downside, but they are essential components of your dog's healthy future. Don't take chances.

Deworming

Your puppy should have been checked and dewormed (if necessary) before coming home with you. Most puppies have worms at some point because some types of worms lie dormant and protected in the dam until hormonal changes caused by her pregnancy activate them and enable them to infect her puppies. Your puppy can also pick up worms from the ground in places where dogs congregate. The best prevention at home is to clean up feces immediately. Some heartworm preventives also prevent many types of worms. Get your puppy regular fecal checks for worms, but don't worm your puppy unnecessarily.

Tapeworms: If you see flat white segments in your dog's stool, she may have tapeworms. Tapeworms are caught when your puppy eats a flea, so the best prevention is flea prevention. Tapeworms require special medication to get rid of them.

Heartworm prevention: Heartworms can kill your dog. They are carried by mosquitoes, so if there is any chance of a single mosquito biting your Eskie, she needs to be on heartworm preventive. Ask your veterinarian when the puppy should begin taking the medication, as it may vary according to your location. Older dogs should be checked for heartworms with a simple blood test before beginning heartworm prevention. Opt for the once-a-month preventive, which is safe and effective.

Spaying and Neutering

Keeping an intact adult is a bother. Males roam, and they go crazy if around a female in estrus. Intact females come in estrus twice a year, starting between six months and one year of age, with each estrus lasting about three

TIP

Vaccinations Don'ts
✔ Do not vaccinate needlessly.
✔ Do not split doses.
✔ Do not vaccinate pregnant dogs.
✔ Do not vaccinate dogs on immunosuppressive therapy.
✔ Do not administer multiple-dose vaccines any more frequently than every two weeks.
✔ Do not vaccinate puppies less than two weeks of age.
✔ Do not end the puppy immunization series before 12 weeks of age.
✔ Do not assume vaccines cannot harm a patient.
✔ Do not use nosodes.

weeks. It is a messy time that can ruin your carpets and furniture, as well as sanity. Breeding puppies is not a casual undertaking. When you consider the dangers of breeding, the work involved in caring for puppies, the expense incurred in raising them, the difficulty of finding good homes, and the lifelong responsibility for each puppy, it's a wonder any sane person chooses to breed.

Intact females are at increased risk of developing pyometra, a potentially fatal infection of the uterus, and of breast cancer. Spaying eliminates the possibility of pyometra, and spaying before the first season drastically reduces the chance of breast cancer. Intact males are more likely to roam or fight, and to develop testicular cancer. Talk to your veterinarian and breeder about the pros and cons of neutering.

Socializing Your Eskie

You have a window of opportunity with your new puppy, a window that will affect her for the rest of her life, a window that will start to inch shut beginning around 12 weeks of age. Like all dogs, Eskies begin life relatively fearless, but gradually become more cautious with age. Eventually they become suspicious of novel situations and objects, adjusting to them with greater difficulty. The secret is to expose your puppy to as much as possible while she's too young to be afraid, then when she meets the same experience later in life she will already know it's nothing to fear. That means exposing her to men, women, children, dogs, cats, traffic, stairs, noises, grooming, leash walking, crates, and alone time.

A curious Eskie can get lost too easily.

Exposing doesn't mean overwhelming. A bad experience is worse than no experience. Good experiences are low stress and involve lots of rewards. And exposure to dogs also entails a chance of exposure to disease. Until your puppy is at least 12 weeks old and has had two sets of puppy vaccinations you should avoid exposing her to strange dogs or places where lots of dogs frequent. That places you in a dilemma—how can you beat that shutting window of opportunity if you can't start to get her out until it's almost too late? You can invite non-dog-owning friends over, or expose her to dogs you know are healthy. Just avoid dog parks and places where lots of strange dogs frequent until she's older.

Children: Children are drawn to cute Eskie puppies, so be sure your puppy isn't mobbed by a crowd of puppy petters. It's best to let your puppy meet children one by one, with both child and puppy on the ground. That way the puppy can't be stepped on or dropped. Children must be taught that puppies can't be handled roughly. Dogs and young children should always be supervised for the well being of both of them.

Being alone: Expose your puppy to being alone. Dogs are not naturally loners, and being alone is stressful for them. It must be done gradually, so your puppy knows you're coming back soon. Give him a special chew toy that you give him only when you're leaving so he will have something to occupy him. Despite your efforts, many dogs will develop separation anxiety. See page 42 for tips on coping with that potentially serious behavioral problem.

The look of relaxed confidence.

Biting: If your Eskie bites somebody, especially a child, the person could be seriously scarred, you will be liable and very likely sued, you will probably not be able to get homeowner's insurance that covers your dog, and your dog may be labeled dangerous, confiscated, and even destroyed. The tendency to snap is partly genetic, and is one reason you want to choose your Eskie from reputable breeders who make temperament a priority. You can work hard to socialize an Eskie that's snippy, and you may be successful, but your best chance is to do it when your Eskie is at the right age to soak in good experiences.

Eskies and Other Pets

If you already have another dog, you should introduce your new Eskie carefully. Let them meet on neutral territory and, if possible, walk them on lead together. Since your puppy probably doesn't know how to walk on lead yet, that may not be possible. In that case keep the older dog on lead but don't allow the puppy to maul him. It may take a week or so for your other dog to warm up to this pesky intruder.

✔ Make sure your older dog always gets fed and petted first, and let him know he is still number one with you.

✔ Lock the puppy away if need be so your older dog gets special time with you.

✔ Feed the older dog special treats so he comes to associate the puppy with good times.

✔ Your puppy will naturally revere your older dog as a minor deity, and your older dog may have to give her some warning growls or snaps to keep her out of his hair. Let him mildly reprimand her if she's out of hand, but try to remove her from him so it doesn't get to that point.

Introduce the family cat in a similar way, except let them meet indoors where she can get out of the way. You may have to crate the puppy at first for her own safety. Eskies and cats can become close friends, but it's mostly up to the cat!

Eskie Exercise

As a youngster, your puppy is the best judge of how much exercise is best. Never force a puppy to go beyond her limits; overexercising young dogs has been linked to several developmental skeletal problems. By the time your puppy becomes an adult, you can begin to work up to longer play periods or walking distances. Regular exercise is absolutely essential to good physical and mental health of your dog; plan on at least 40 minutes each day, rain or shine. Walking is an excellent and safe form of exercise; running carries more risks of injury.

Weather Extremes

Winter

There are few more breathtaking sights than an Eskie frolicking in the freshly driven snow. It will come as no surprise that Eskimo Dogs like the cold! But even these little snowmen have their limits, and should not be left in extremely cold weather without insulated shelter.

✔ Dogs with hair loss problems should wear a coat.

✔ Freezing weather brings other hazards. As your Eskie romps in the snow, check her feet regularly. Balls of frozen snow accumulate

---

TIP

Keep It Cool

Even if all your dog does is loll in the yard all day, you must provide shade and plenty of cool water to offset heatstroke. Some Eskie owners set up a fan in a safe location, and many provide a child's wading pool filled with water. Incidentally, shaving your Eskie does little, if anything, to improve her cooling capabilities, although removing as much of the undercoat as possible will help. A shaved dog is subject to sunburn and fly bites, and besides, looks so very un-Eskie!

---

between the toes and become very uncomfortable; these can be avoided by coating the dog's feet with oil or butter before the walk, or by having the dog wear booties.

✔ Walking on streets treated with salt will also be irritating to the paw pads, so be sure to rinse them upon returning home.

✔ Some winter threats can be more deadly. Dogs do not understand that the ice on frozen lakes can break, so you must be vigilant when around thin ice.

✔ Be aware of metal items in your yard. Puppies love to lick, and they will lick everything; licking metal in freezing weather is as bad an idea for dogs as it is for people.

Summer

Summer has its own list of caveats, the most obvious of which is heat.

Heatstroke: Many dogs have died of heatstroke because their owners wanted to have them along on a trip, and then left them unattended in a poorly ventilated car. Many did not intend to leave them so long, but when they got into the store there was a long line, and in the air-conditioned comfort of the store they lost contact with just how hot it was outside—not to mention, inside a closed car. Heatstroke also occurs as a result of another well-intentioned owner mistake: taking the dog for a walk or run in the summer sun. Dogs do not have sweat glands, and must cool themselves through evaporation from the tongue. This system is not as effective as the human system, and dogs can be overcome by heat when their owners are scarcely affected. Unless you are taking your dog for a swim, leave her at home in the daytime and schedule your outings for early morning or evening.

Your active Eskie can overdo activities in hot weather.

Insects: With summer also come insect bites and stings. Watch the edges of the ears for fly bites, which can cause a problem. Better yet, use an insect repellent if your dog must stay outside for long periods. If your dog is stung, remove the stinger and watch to make sure there is no allergic reaction.

Fireworks: Summer carries another potentially dangerous event: the Fourth of July. Every year city shelters are filled with lost dogs that fled in terror from noisy fireworks. Many dogs are not claimed, and many are struck in traffic. Secure your dog on this occasion, and also during thunderstorms.

Car Manners

The ideal way for your Eskie to travel is in a crate in your car. Still, not all pet owners can carry crates in their car, but there are doggy seat belts available from pet supply catalogs or pet shops. At any rate, your dog should be taught to sit or lie down quietly in the car. She should never hang her head out the window, where bugs and debris can injure her eyes. And owners who allow their dogs to ride loose in the back of pickups might as well buy a bumper sticker stating "Moron on Board" because that's what they're advertising.

Good Fences Make Good Neighbors

Your Eskie would probably love to visit all your neighbors to help them with their gardening and exercising their cats and all sorts of things that you may think are cute and that your neighbor will find annoying. Your dog

Even Eskies require extra care when playing in ice and snow.

should never, *ever* be allowed to roam the streets on her own. Not only is it dangerous for the dog, but it will make both of you extremely unpopular. Few items can raise the ire of home owners more than dog feces on their lawn, and with good reason. Other people should not be expected to take on your responsibility of cleaning up after your dog. Nor should other people be expected to listen to your dog bark incessantly. As your neighborhood Eskie ambassador, please be an asset to dogdom and to Eskies in particular, and make your dog a good neighbor.

Boarding

Sometimes you have no choice but to leave your Eskie behind when you travel, and may need to board your dog at a kennel or at your veterinarian's. Ask friends for recommendations. The ideal kennel will have climate-controlled accommodations, preferably indoor/outdoor runs. Make an unannounced visit to the kennel and ask to see the facilities. Although you can't expect spotlessness and a perfumy atmosphere, runs should be clean and the odor should not be overpowering. All dogs should have clean water and proper bedding.

Your dog may be more comfortable if a pet-sitter comes to your home and feeds and exercises her regularly.

Don't forget your dog's breeders, who may welcome a visit from their former baby, and your Eskie may feel more at home there. But be sure that the facilities are safe and escape-proof in case your Eskie decides she wants to go home. Whatever means you choose, always leave emergency numbers and your veterinarian's name.

Lost Dog

If your little friend escapes or gets lost, you must act quickly in order to ensure her safe return. If she has recently escaped, don't wait for her to return. Immediately go to the very worst place you could imagine her going. If you live near a highway, go there, and search backward toward your home. Be certain, however, that your dog does not find you first and follow you to the highway! And if you are driving, be certain that you do not drive recklessly and endanger your own dog's life should she return to you.

✔ If you still can't find your Eskie, get pictures of Eskies and go door to door.

✔ Ask any workers or delivery persons in the area.

✔ Call the local animal control, police department, and veterinarians.

✔ Make up *large* posters with a picture of an Eskimo dog.

✔ Take out an ad in the local paper.

✔ Mention a reward, but do not specify an amount.

Caution: Never give anyone money before seeing your dog. There are a number of scams involving answering lost dog ads, many asking for money for shipping the dog back to you from a distance or for paying veterinarian bills, when very often these people have not really

TIP

Identification

Tattoos: Your Eskie should always wear a collar with identification, but even that isn't always enough. You can have your social security number or your dog's AKC number tattooed on her inner thigh; this is an especially good option to have done when your dog is under anesthesia, such as when she is being spayed.

Microchips: A high-tech but very affordable option is a microchip, a rice-sized pellet that is injected under the skin over the shoulders. It takes only a second for your veterinarian to do this. Most veterinarians and shelters own scanners that read the data from the chip; that information will include contact numbers for you should your dog be found.

found your dog. If your dog is tattooed, you can have the person read the tattoo to you in order to positively identify your pet. Other scammers actually steal your dog for reward money, and wait until you are desperate and will pay a high reward, and then have been known to also burglarize your home when you go to meet their partner to pick up the dog! The moral: Protect your dog in the first place from theft or loss, and be wary when asked for money in return for your dog.

You can help your relationship with your dog by understanding his nature, and by helping him to understand yours.

The Eskie's World

When you share your world with a dog, you may live in the same place, but you don't experience the same world.

Your world is dominated by the visual experience, filled with colors and details. Your dog cannot see the fine details that you can, nor can he appreciate the rich array of colors.

Colors: Dogs can see colors, but their sense of color is like that of what we commonly refer to as a "color-blind" person. That is, they confuse similar shades of yellow-green, yellow, orange, and red, but can see and discriminate blue, indigo, and violet from all other colors.

Smell: A dog's sense of smell is thousands of times more acute than yours. The next time you become impatient when your dog wants to sniff something on a walk, consider it the same as when you stop to admire a sunset.

An Eskie is never too young or too old to learn.

Taste: Dogs also have a well-developed sense of taste, and have most of the same taste receptors that people do. Research has shown that they prefer meat and although there are many individual differences, the average dog prefers beef, pork, lamb, chicken, and horsemeat, in that order.

Hearing: Dogs can hear much higher tones than can humans, and so can be irritated by high hums from your TV or from those ultrasonic flea collars. The Eskie's pricked ears are unencumbered by heavy fur and are ideally suited for detecting and localizing sounds.

Part of the Family

If you expect your Eskie to be part of the family, show him what is expected of a family member. Because dogs are pack animals, family life is very natural for them. Your family will be your dog's pack now, and just as puppies in a pack look to their mother and the older pack members for leadership, your puppy will look to

Education is about mutual respect and bonding.

every good Eskie trainer should follow, and some commands every good Eskie should know.

What Every Good Eskie Trainer Should Know

Before trying to train your Eskie, you must train yourself. Be patient in the face of sessions that seem to make no progress, calm in the presence of an Eskie determined to do just the opposite of what you desire, jolly in the midst of failure, and clearheaded in the eye of an Eskie storm. You must be consistent, firm, gentle, and realistic.

Name first: The first ingredient in any command is your dog's name. You probably spend a good deal of your day talking, with very few words intended as commands for your dog. So warn your dog that this talk is directed toward him. Say his name first, then follow with a command, and finally help him perform that command.

Then command: Many trainers make the mistake of simultaneously saying the command word *at the same time* that they are guiding the dog into position. *This is incorrect.* The command comes immediately *before* the desired action or position. The crux of training is anticipation: the dog comes to anticipate that after hearing a command, if he performs some action, he will be rewarded. When the command and action come at the same time, the command word loses its predictive value for the dog. Again, the sequence is name, then command, and then action. You should not have to shout commands, nor repeat them over and over.

you for leadership. Don't let him down. Your puppy naturally assumes you're the boss unless you convince him otherwise.

Intelligence

Many a circus-goer in the early 1900s marveled at the uncanny intelligence and agility of the striking white Eskimo dogs as they regularly performed intricate and sometimes dangerous tricks under the big top. Many of these performers can be found in the pedigrees of modern American Eskimo Dogs. So have confidence in your Eskie's ability to learn—he's from the right stuff!

Perhaps the greatest evidence of the dog's intelligence is his ability to learn in spite of many of the commonly employed but totally illogical training methods in use. Although no two dogs are alike—and certainly no two American Eskimo Dogs—there are some rules that

Equipment

Equipment for training should include a 4- to 6-foot (1.2–1.8 m) nylon, web, or leather lead (never chain), a longer lightweight line of about 20 feet (6 m), and either a buckle collar or slip (choke) collar. The latter has a truly unfortunate name, as it should never be used to choke your Eskie.

Note: The slip collar should never remain tight on your dog's neck; if it does, you're using it wrong.

The lead is attached to the ring that goes through the other ring; this is placed on the dog so that the ring with the lead attached comes up around the left side of the dog's neck. If put on backward, it will not release itself after being tightened (because you will be on the right side of your dog for most training).

Higher Education

You may find that you and your Eskimo Dog enjoy training sessions; in fact, you may be thinking of your Eskie as "gifted." Perhaps you would like to learn more, or be able to practice around dogs , or discuss problems with people who have similar interests.

✔ Most cities have obedience clubs that conduct classes. Many include puppy kindergarten classes so that young dogs can be properly socialized.

✔ Some clubs will advertise in the newspaper or phone book, but you can also contact the American Kennel Club or your local Humane Society for the name of the club nearest you.

✔ You might also contact one of the American Eskimo Dog breed clubs and ask for names of Eskie obedience enthusiasts in your area.

✔ Attend a local obedience trial (contact the AKC for date and location) and ask local owners of

TIP

Choke Collar

The choke collar should *never* be left on your Eskie after a training session; there are too many tragic cases where a choke collar really did earn its name after being snagged on a fence, bush, or even a playmate's tooth.

happy working dogs (especially Eskies!) where they train. Be aware that not all trainers may understand the Eskimo psyche, and not all classes may be right for you and your Eskimo Dog.

Pesky Eskies

Asking Eskie owners about their dogs' behavior problems is like asking doting parents about their child prodigies' behavior problems—you don't get a lot of answers! Remember, Eskies are still dogs and share the behavioral problems to which all dogs are prone.

Jumping Up

Although it may seem so cute when your baby Eskie puts his paws on your leg, your guests will probably not appreciate your full-grown Eskie jumping on their new clothes or on their children.

✔ The simplest solution is to avoid the problem in puppies by crouching down so that your face is at a level that does not require the dog to jump up.

✔ When you are standing, a quick step backward so that the puppy's feet meet only air is often sufficient discouragement.

TIP

Training Tips
✔ Teach your dog with kindness and rewards, not force and punishment.

✔ Teach new skills in a quiet place away from distractions. Only when he knows the skill very well should you gradually start practicing it in other places.

✔ Don't try to train your dog if he's tired, hot, or has just eaten. You want him peppy and hungry for your treats.

✔ Don't train your dog if you're impatient or angry.

✔ Always train in gradual steps. Give rewards for getting closer and closer to the final trick. Be patient!

✔ Give a click (see HOW-TO: Clicker Training Your Eskie, page 48) instantly when your dog does what you want. The faster you click, the easier it is for your dog to figure out what you like.

✔ Give a reward as soon as you can after the click.

✔ Don't forget to praise and pet your dog as part of the reward!

✔ Just say a cue word once. Repeating it over and over won't help your dog learn it.

✔ Once your dog has learned the completed trick and is doing it consistently, you don't have to click your approval anymore. But you still need to tell him he's good and give him a reward.

✔ Dogs learn better in short sessions. Train your dog for only about 10 to 15 minutes at a time. Always quit while he's still having fun. You can train him several times a day if you want.

✔ Try to end your training sessions doing something your dog can do well. You want to end on a high note!

✔ Older dogs can be told to sit and stay while greeting the owner or guests.

✔ A highly excitable dog may be distracted by a thrown ball.

✔ All too often dogs are banished to the yard permanently because they insist on jumping on people; unfortunately, the isolated dog will be so thrilled when he is visited by his owner that the jumping up behavior will only get worse.

Barking

Barking is a natural and useful trait of dogs, and Eskies are natural watchdogs. But the surest way to make your neighbors dislike your Eskie is to let him bark excessively. Allow your Eskie to bark momentarily at strangers, and then call him to you and praise him for quiet behavior. The best watchdogs sound the alarm, seek out the owner, and then await the owner's directions.

Seeking attention: Puppies that are isolated will often bark for attention and alleviating loneliness. Even if the attention includes punishment, the puppy will continue to bark to get the temporary presence of the owner.

Solution: Move the dog's bed to a less isolated location. If this is not possible, the pup's quiet behavior must be rewarded by the owner's presence, working up to gradually longer and longer periods. The distraction of a special chew toy, given only at bedtime, may help alleviate barking. The puppy that must spend the day in the yard alone is a greater challenge. Again, the simplest solution is to change the situation, perhaps by adding another dog or pet, or by giving him interactive toys.

Chewing

One of the best things about owning an American Eskimo Dog is the joyous greeting you receive upon your return home. But this heartwarming reunion can be greatly cooled by the sight of your home in shambles. Home destruction accounts for more dogs being exiled to the yard, or worse, the pound, than any other behavioral problem. But given proper training, your Eskie and your furniture can learn to coexist peacefully.

Solution: Puppies chew. Your job is to see to it that they don't chew forbidden articles. A variety of chew toys will save you many dollars in sod, shoes, and furniture—as long as you still monitor the puppy so that he never digs or chews the wrong things.

Adult dogs may dig or destroy items through frustration or boredom. The best way to deal with these dogs is to provide both physical interaction (chasing a ball) and mental interaction (practicing a few simple obedience commands) daily.

Home Destruction

If you've ever returned home to a scene of household demolition, the first thing that crossed your mind probably wasn't "Gee, my dog sure does love me." But sadly, that's exactly what he's

TIP

Reading Your Eskie

You must become part naturalist in order to fully appreciate your dog's language.
✔ What does it mean when your Eskie greets you with a wagging tail and lips pulled back? Most people would think the dog was snarling, but when combined with a happy, submissive greeting, this facial expression is actually known as a "submissive grin."
✔ What if your dog is lowering his body, wagging his tail, holding his tail down, holding his ears down, urinating, and even rolling over? These are all signs of submissive behavior.
✔ What if the dog greeted you with lips pulled back, but with a high, rigidly held tail, hackles raised, perched on his toes, with a stiff-legged gait, a direct stare, forward pricked ears, and perhaps lifting his leg to mark a tree? These are all signs of dominant, threatening behavior. This dog is, indeed, snarling, and you had better leave him alone. Approaching or punishing this dog would likely result in a dog bite.
✔ What if the dog greeted you with lips pulled back, maybe a little growl, a wagging tail, and his front legs and elbows on the ground and rear in the air? This is the classic "play-bow" position, and is an invitation for a game. Take your friend up on it!

saying. You are your dog's pack, and dogs don't do well when separated from their pack. Spiting you is the last thing on their mind, yet it's the first thing that comes to their owner's mind.

Separation anxiety: Fixing this problem, called separation anxiety, will take time and effort.

✔ Downplay your departures and returns.

✔ Ignore the dog for 30 minutes before leaving, and if you give him attention, do it only when he is not trying to solicit attention from you.

✔ Reward him for being calm.

✔ Teach him to ignore your pre-departure cues, such as putting on your shoes or picking up the keys, by doing that randomly throughout the day without going anywhere.

✔ Teach him instead a "safety signal," such as an air freshener spray, that will mean to him you're coming right back.

✔ Spray the spray, then leave for 30 seconds and return. This signal is his assurance that you'll be right back. Don't use it early in training if you plan to be gone all day.

"Sit!"

✔ Gradually build up time, never allowing the dog to be alone long enough to get stressed. Repeat this exercise about 10 times a day. When you return, ignore the dog until he is calm, and then reward him for doing a simple trick.

Although separation anxiety is the most common cause of home destruction, it's not the only one. Puppies can leave a trail of destruction. Confine them to a safe place, and give them a special toy, preferably an interactive one that takes the dog lots of time to extract treats from. Other dogs may pull down curtains because they see something they want to chase outside the window, or they may dig in an effort to hide from something, such as a thunderstorm, that scares them.

Fears: Like people, dogs can be afraid of illogical things. High on the list are loud noises. These fears can be difficult to deal with because once you realize the dog has a problem, it's usually well-ingrained. Your veterinarian can prescribe antianxiety drugs to give during training or storms, which will help if you give them quickly enough. Dog-appeasing pheromones and antianxiety wraps may also help.

Many dogs are afraid of other dogs or strangers. The best cure is prevention with lots of socialization as a young puppy. As an adult, the best treatment is to gradually expose the dog to other dogs or strangers. Reward your dog for doing a trick in front of other dogs and people. Gradually move closer. The people or dogs should ignore your dog. Eventually you should be able to walk your dog on leash alongside another dog, and to let your dog sniff a strange person and accept a treat from that person.

Never overwhelm a dog with what he is afraid of; it only makes it worse. Always go in slow, gradual steps, teaching the dog to be confident at one level before moving to the next.

Digging: All dogs dig; Eskies just happen to have a talent for it. You won't be able to stop this behavior easily, so the best alternative is to redirect it to his own sandbox. Designate a small area as his, possibly filling it with sand. Seed it with toys and treasures every few days to encourage digging there. If he digs elsewhere, take him to his area.

House Soiling

When a dog soils the house, several questions must be asked. The first is obvious: Was the dog ever really completely house-trained? If not, you must begin house-training anew (see House-training Your Eskie, page 25). Sometimes a house-trained dog will be forced to soil the house because of a bout of diarrhea, and afterward will continue to soil in the same area. If this happens, restrict that area from the dog, and revert to basic house-training lessons once again.

✔ Submissive dogs may urinate upon greeting you; punishment only makes this "submissive urination" worse. Keep greetings calm, don't bend over or otherwise dominate the dog, and usually this can be outgrown.

✔ Some dogs defecate or urinate due to the stress of separation anxiety; you must treat the anxiety (see Chewing, page 41) to cure the symptom.

✔ Older dogs may simply not have the bladder control that they had as youngsters; paper training or a doggy door is the best solution for them.

✔ Older spayed females may "dribble"; ask your veterinarian about drug therapy, which may help.

✔ Even younger dogs may have lost control due to an infection; several small urine spots are a sign that a trip to the veterinarian is needed.

✔ Male dogs may "lift their leg" inside of the house as a means of marking it as theirs. Castration will solve this problem; otherwise, diligent deodorizing and the use of some dog-deterring odorants (available at pet stores) may help.

"Heel!"

Escaping and Roaming

Keeping your Eskie in an enclosed area not only makes it a more welcome neighbor, but also an Eskie with a longer life expectancy. But sometimes your Eskie doesn't see it that way. It is more enticing to visit the local schoolyard, go calling on a lady dog, or hang out with his stray buddies. Find out the reason for your dog's travels. If it is for human or canine interaction, arrange to spend more time with your Eskie and for your Eskie to have supervised play with a canine friend. The male that roams looking for females can be effectively cured by castration. Although it is tempting to punish the roamer when caught, in the long run this is counterproductive as dogs may learn that coming to you results in punishment.

Prevention: The most effective cure is prevention, by making a yard that is escape-proof from the very beginning. Many dogs are actually inadvertently taught to escape by their owners.

"Come!"

Fences: First enclosures are often adequate for young puppies, but as the puppy grows, the enclosure can no longer contain him. At this point, many owners make some sort of minimal repair, such as increasing the fence height by a few inches. With a little more effort, the Eskie clears this height. Another few inches are added, until, a few inches at a time, the frustrated owner finally realizes that he has coached his Eskie to Olympic jumping abilities. If you wanted your Eskie to learn to jump high fences, wouldn't you build up to it a little at a time? Then why use the same tactic to teach your dog *not* to scale high fences?

If you want your dog to stay in the yard, make the yard Eskie-proof from the very beginning.

Fearfulness

A gregarious breed by nature, nonetheless, the American Eskimo Dog is somewhat conservative with strangers, and there may be times when your Eskie may act shy or fearful. Your Eskie should never be pushed into situations that might overwhelm him. A program of gradual desensitization, with the dog exposed to the frightening person or thing and then rewarded for calm behavior, is time-consuming but the best way to alleviate the fear. Never force a dog that is afraid of strangers to be petted by somebody he doesn't know; it in no way helps the dog overcome his fear and is a good way for the stranger to get bitten. Strangers should be asked to ignore shy dogs, even when approached by the dog. Dogs seem to fear the attention of a stranger more than they fear the strangers themselves.

Eskies are as varied in size as they are in abilities.

It is always useful if your Eskie knows a few simple commands; performing these exercises correctly gives you a reason to praise the dog and also increases the dog's sense of security because he knows what is expected of him. In any attempt to overcome fear, the most important rules are also the most tempting to break: never hurry, and never push the dog to the point that he is afraid.

Aggression

No matter what size Eskie you own, his teeth are large enough to do considerable damage. The best cure for aggression is prevention, and the best prevention is to carefully select your Eskie from a responsible breeder. Poorly bred

Eskies have developed a reputation as an untrustworthy breed, but knowledgeable breeders have worked hard to develop trustworthy companions. Truly aggressive well-bred Eskies

TIP

Smaller Varieties of Eskies

The smaller varieties of Eskimo Dogs are not as well suited for young children; because the mini and toy Eskies can be more easily hurt by rough play, they may become aggressive out of self-defense.

With well-conducted training, your Eskie is unlikely to develop aggression-related problems.

are very rare, and in most cases the cause can be traced to one of several family situations.

Reasons and solutions:

✔ Some Eskies may bite out of fear, perhaps because the owner is pulling them by the collar to a feared location. The solution is to find out what the dog is afraid of and use the gradual desensitization method outlined previously. Be aware that unlike in humans, where direct eye contact is seen as a sign of sincerity, staring a dog directly in the eye is interpreted by the dog as a threat. It can cause a fearful dog to bite out of what he perceives as self-defense.

✔ Eskies have an innate tendency to defend their territory; however, they should not threaten guests you have welcomed into your home. Teach your Eskie to look forward to guests by rewarding proper behavior, such as sitting and staying, in the guests' presence.

✔ Some dogs will bite out of resentment. Again, the solution is to teach your Eskie to respond to simple commands such as *sit* and *stay*, and use them as needed. In drastic cases, attention can be withheld from the dog except in the presence of stress, so that the dog associates them with triggers, something that brings him attention and rewards.

✔ Any dog that is socially isolated is more apt to become aggressive; and, once aggressive, more apt to be kept isolated.

✔ Perhaps the most common cause of aggression is the practice of some pet owners to tie out their dogs. A dog that is tied out with a view of the family having a good time becomes frustrated at not being able to join in; this frustration eventually often vents itself as aggression. Reconsider getting an Eskie if you do not intend to make it a real part of your family.

✔ Some cases of aggression occur when a dominant dog believes his owner to be his subordinate; when the owner tells him to do something, he refuses, and if pushed, may bite. Such behavior is rare in Eskies, but can happen if an owner has not established a proper leadership role. Always allowing the dog to have his way, allowing him to lead on walks, feeding him on demand, petting him for no reason—all of these actions can lead the dominant-type dog to conclude that he is the leader of the pack. Owners must stop these behaviors, and establish themselves as leaders by the use of obedience exercises.

✔ Aggression toward other dogs or animals is also uncommon in Eskimo Dogs. It most often arises through territorial (in the case of strange dogs) or dominance (in the case of familiar dogs) disputes. When you walk your Eskimo Dog down the street and he urinates on the trees lining the way, your pet is marking his territory. When the neighbor's dog does the same thing, both dogs mistakenly believe that street to be their territory—and when they meet, they may fight for it.

✔ More problematic is the case where two dogs that live together do not get along. Dogs may be vying for dominance, and fights will occur until one dog emerges as the clear victor. But even in cases where one dog is dominant, fights may erupt when both are competing for the owner's attention. The dominant dog expects to get that attention before the subordinate, but being a fair-minded owner, you may tend to give attention equally, or to even favor the "underdog." This can be interpreted by the dominant dog as an uprising by the subordinate dog, who is then attacked. This is one case where playing favorites (to the dominant dog) will actually be a favor to the subordinate dog in the long run!

Coprophagia: Even Good Dogs Eat Bad Things

Stool eating: Many explanations have been advanced (and discarded) for why what is so vile to us is so enticing to them; whatever the reason, it is still scant consolation the next time your Eskie tries to kiss you after indulging! But don't be ashamed if your Eskie grabs a forbidden morsel; it is very common. Just do your best to keep feces out of reach and realize that dogs aren't quite as human as you would like to believe!

Less tolerable is the dog that eats his own feces. A number of theories have been advanced to explain this most repulsive of eating habits, but none is adequate to explain all instances. Food additives can make the stool less savory, but the best cure is prevention by cleanliness. Many dogs experiment with feces eating as puppies, but most grow out of it.

When All Else Fails

Chances are you and your Eskie will live together blissfully with never a major behavioral problem. But if a problem does arise that you are unable to solve, consult your veterinarian. Some problems have physiological bases that can be treated. Also, your veterinarian may refer you to a specialist in canine behavior problems.

Dog training has taken an incredible leap forward since the old push-and-jerk methods of years ago. The methods aren't really new; they're the same ones used by professional trainers for decades. But only recently have pet trainers realized the value of these methods. They produce happy, well-trained dogs that are eager to learn more.

Reward-based Training

The secret is in reward-based training. For dogs, the reward can be a treat, a toy, or even your praise. When your Eskie is rewarded for doing something, he will want to do it again.

Punishment

Punishment isn't a good way to teach a dog to do anything. About the only thing it's good for is to teach a dog to do nothing!

When the front goes up, the rear goes down.

Clickers

Your puppy doesn't understand people rules or language. He hears many words, few directed to him, so he learns to tune most of them out. To make your dog pay attention, use a sound he doesn't normally hear. Serious trainers use a clicker, an inexpensive device available at pet stores that clicks when pressed. The clicker signals *"Good!"* and is always followed by a reward.

Click immediately when your dog does what you want; it marks the event and tells the dog, "Yes, that's it!" Then reward and praise as soon as you can after the click. Once your dog responds reliably you don't have to keep clicking "That's it!" but you must still praise and reward him.

Note: No dog learns to do something perfectly at first. Teach him gradually, shaping his behavior closer and closer to what you want. By following the click with a reward, your dog tries to repeat what he did for the click.

Sit

You'll need a way to make a click sound and many, many tiny treats. The simplest way is to help your dog find out how to make you click without forcing him into position. Hold the treat just above and behind his nose, so he must bend his

rear legs to look up at it. Click and reward. Repeat several times, gradually moving the treat further back so he bends his legs more until he sits. Click and reward each time he gets closer, and soon he'll be racing to drop his rear.

When he sits reliably to the lure, introduce a cue word: *"Bobby, sit."* Say it just before luring him into position, then gradually fade out use of the treat, using just your hand at first, then nothing. You can also teach him to sit by pushing his rear down, but this method teaches your Eskie that he can figure out how to make you click, priming him for other learning more easily.

Down

With your Eskie sitting, use your treat to lure his nose down and forward. You may have to prevent him from walking forward by gently restraining him with your other hand on his withers. Click and reward for just putting his nose down and forward, then for reaching to the ground, then for lowering his elbows, then for lying all the way down. Once he's doing that, click and reward only for doing it when you give the cue *"Bobby, down!"* Congratulations! You've taught your Eskie to lie down without a struggle.

YOUR ESKIE

Stay

So far you've used the click to tell your dog he's doing right, and once he hears the click he's allowed to get up. Now with him in a *sit* or *down*, wait a few seconds after he's in position before clicking and rewarding. Tell him *"Stay"* and gradually lengthen the time he must stay before getting the click and reward. It's better for him to succeed than to fail, so don't push him. If he gets up, simply put him back in position and have him stay a shorter time.

Heel

Old methods to train a dog to heel advised you to jerk the dog's choke collar when he got out of position. It hardly seemed fair, especially since most people didn't show their dogs what was expected of them beforehand. Clicker training makes it easier.

To have your dog walk abreast of your left leg, you must get there gradually. If your dog isn't leash trained, place him on a leash and walk with him. Click and reward when he's by your side. Show him a treat and encourage him to walk a few feet with you for it. Click and reward. Work up to slightly longer distances. If he resists, go in a different direction. Soon he will learn that walking by your side makes you a clicking snack dispenser.

If he insists on pulling you down the sidewalk, it's possible he sees something he wants more than a treat. In that case turn away from what he wants and have him heel. Once he does, click and reward by saying *"OK"* and letting him investigate. Gradually require him to walk a few steps toward the object without pulling before giving him his click and *"OK."*

Come

Your Eskie already knows how to come when he sees you serving his dinner. You must make

An Eskie in proper heeling position moves in step alongside but out of the way of the handler.

him want to come that eagerly every time you call him. Do this by making it rewarding to come to you. Keep some treats—and your clicker—handy, and be generous when he comes. Even if he's been up to mischief, be sure not to reprimand him when he comes; Eskies will figure out they'd be better off staying away next time.

With a helper, you can play a game that will get your Eskie really running to you. In an enclosed area have your friend hold your puppy while you show him a treat or toy. Back away, enticing him until he's struggling to get to you. Then call out *"Bobby come!"* and turn and run away just as your friend releases him. As he gets to you click, and reward. Make a game out of running faster and farther from him. Always quit while he still wants to play.

You need not limit yourself to the standard *sit, down, stay, heel,* and *come.* Remember, Eskies can learn just about any circus trick. You can teach your Eskie a real repertoire, all using the same basic shape, click, and reward concept.

AMERICAN ESKIMO DOG NUTRITION

A balanced diet must have minimal amounts of protein, fat, carbohydrates, vitamins, minerals, and water.

"You are what you eat" is just as true for dogs as it is for people. Because your Eskie can't go shopping for her dinner, she "will be what you feed her," so you have total responsibility for feeding your dog a high-quality balanced diet that will enable her to live a long and active life. Dog food claims can be conflicting and confusing, but there are some guidelines that you can follow.

Food Choices

Commercial dog foods should meet the Association of American Feed Control Officials' (AAFCO) guidelines for whatever group of dogs the food is aimed toward. Almost all commercially available foods have a statement on the container certifying that the food meets AAFCO guidelines. Critics contend that these guidelines

Fueling an active Eskie requires a balanced diet.

are too lenient, and that many pet foods are made from substandard ingredients. Premium dog foods, available from large pet supply chains, usually use better-quality ingredients and exceed AAFCO minimums.

Varieties

Commercial foods come in dry, canned, and moist varieties.
• Dry foods are generally healthiest, provide needed chewing action, are most economical, but tend to be less appealing. Many people mix them with tastier canned foods.
• Canned foods are usually higher in fat and are tastier.
• Semimoist foods are high in sugar and, although handy for travel, lack the better attributes of the other food types.

Note: Dog treats may not always meet AAFCO requirements for a complete diet but are fine as supplements.

Good nutrition begins in puppyhood and lasts a lifetime.

Home-prepared Diets

Home-prepared diets have become increasingly popular. Such diets have the advantage of being fresh and of using human-grade ingredients. If they are prepared according to recipes devised by certified canine nutritionists, they should have the correct proportion of nutrients. Unlike commercial dog foods, such diets are not customarily tested on generations of dogs, which makes them vulnerable to looking healthy on paper but not being properly digested or utilized. They can also be labor-intensive, although large batches can be made and frozen.

BARF Diet

Some people prefer to feed their dogs a BARF (Bones And Raw Food) diet, with the idea that such a diet better emulates that of a wild dog. They point out that nobody ever sees wolves eating from a bag of kibble, or even cooking their catch of the day. These people feed raw meaty bones along with vegetables. Although dogs have better resistance to bacterial food poisoning than humans do, such diets have nonetheless occasionally been associated with food poisoning in dogs. Commercially available meats may be awash in contaminated liquids. Perhaps the most serious problem with the BARF diets, however, is that most people who claim to use them never bother to find a nutritionally balanced diet, but instead rely on friends who advocate a solid diet of chicken wings or some equally unbalanced diet.

Nutrition

Your Eskie's nutritional needs are best met by a diet rich in meat that also contains some vegetable matter. Meat is tastier, higher in protein, and more digestible (meaning smaller stools and fewer gas problems) than plant-based ingredients. A rule of thumb is that at least three of the first six ingredients of a dog food should be animal-derived.

Protein: Protein provides the building blocks for bone, muscle, coat, and antibodies. Eggs, followed by meats, have higher-quality and more digestible proteins than plant-derived proteins.

Fat: Fat adds taste, provides energy, and aids in the transport of vitamins. Too little fat in the diet causes dry coats and scaly skin. Too much fat can cause diarrhea, obesity, and a reduced appetite for more nutritious foods.

Carbohydrates: Carbohydrates from plants and grains aren't well utilized by dogs unless they are cooked. Carbohydrates from rice are best utilized, followed by potato and corn, then wheat, oats, and beans. Excessive carbohydrates in the diet can cause diarrhea, flatulence, and poor athletic performance.

Vitamins: Vitamins are essential for normal life functions. Dogs require vitamins A, D, E, B1, B2, and B12, plus niacin, pyridoxine, pantothenic acid, folic acid, and choline. Most dog foods have these vitamins added in their optimal percentages, so that supplementing with vitamin tablets is seldom necessary.

Minerals: Minerals help build tissues and organs, and are part of many body fluids and enzymes. Deficiencies or excesses can cause anemia, poor growth, appetite for nonfoods, fractures, convulsions, vomiting, weakness, heart problems, and many other disorders. Again, most commercial dog foods have minerals added in their ideal percentages. It is seldom a good idea to supplement your dog's diet with minerals.

Fiber: Fiber, such as beet pulp or rice bran, should make up a small part of the dog's diet. It's often used in weight-loss diets to give the

TIP

Percentage of Nutrients

The percentage of each nutrient that's best for your dog depends on your dog's age and health. Growing dogs need more protein, active dogs need more protein and fat, fat dogs need more protein and less fat, and sick dogs need reduction or addition of various ingredients according to their illnesses.

dog a full feeling, although its effectiveness is controversial. Too much fiber can cause large stool volume and can prevent the digestion of other nutrients.

Water: Water is essential for life. It dissolves and transports other nutrients, helps regulate body temperature, and helps lubricate joints.

Dogs that spend time in the cold burn—and need—more calories.

Dehydration can cause or complicate many health problems. Keep a bowl of clean, cool water available for your dog at all times.

Follow Your Dog's Preferences

Finally, let your Eskie help you choose.
✔ Find a food that your dog likes, one that creates a small volume of firm stool and results in good weight with a full coat.
✔ Be aware of the signs of possible food allergies (loss of hair, scratching, inflamed ears).

Food Changing

You may have to experiment to find just the right food. One of the great mysteries of life is why the dog, renowned for its lead stomach and preference to eat out of garbage cans, can at the same time develop violently upset stomachs simply from changing from one high-quality dog food to another. But it happens. So when changing foods do so gradually, mixing in progressively more and more of the new food each day for several days.

How Much, How Often?

Very young puppies should be fed three or four times a day, on a regular schedule. Feed them as much as they care to eat in about 15 minutes. From the age of three to six months, puppies should be fed three times daily, and after that, twice daily. Adult dogs can be fed once a day, but it is actually preferable to feed smaller meals twice a day. A geriatric dog will especially benefit from several small meals rather than one large one. Some people let the dog decide when to eat by leaving dry food

TIP

What Not to Feed

Although too many table scraps can throw off the nutrient balance, recent research has found that dogs that eat table scraps in addition to their regular commercial diet have less incidence of gastric torsion (see page 66). But choose your scraps carefully. Avoid any cooked bone, which can splinter or cause impaction. Avoid chunks of fat, which can bring on pancreatitis, and avoid the following human foods that are toxic to dogs:
✔ Onions cause a condition in which the red blood cells are destroyed. Eating an entire onion could be fatal to a small dog.
✔ Chocolate contains theobromine, which can cause death in dogs.
✔ Macadamia nuts cause some dogs to get very ill; the cause is not understood.
✔ Raisins and grapes have been associated with kidney failure in some dogs.

available at all times. If you choose to let the dog "self-feed," monitor her weight to be sure she is not overindulging.

Proper Weight

Proper Eskie weight is in the range of 5 to 7 pounds (2.3–3.2 kg) for toys, 10 to 20 pounds (4.5–9.1 kg) for minis, 25 to 35 pounds (11.3–15.9 kg) for standards. You should be able to just feel the ribs slightly when you run your hands along the rib cage; in addition, when wet, there should be an indication of a

Special Diets

Several diseases can be helped by feeding specially formulated diets, whether home-made or commercially available. By understanding what ingredients must be avoided in a particular illness, you may be able to include some treats in the diet as well.

Food allergies: Food allergies are usually signaled by itchy skin and ears, and sometimes by gastrointestinal upset. Such allergies are usually triggered by particular proteins, so by feeding only proteins the dog has never eaten before, such as venison, duck, or rabbit, the allergic symptoms should subside. If they do, ingredients are added back one by one until an ingredient is found that triggers the response. Some hypoallergenic diets consist not of novel proteins, but of protein molecules that are too small to cause allergic reactions.

Urinary stones: Dogs that tend to form urinary stones may be helped by diets high in fiber and certain minerals. Because there are several types of urinary stones, your

veterinarian can suggest which diet is appropriate.

Diabetes mellitus: Diabetic dogs need diets high in complex carbohydrates, and they need to be fed on a strict schedule.

Liver disease: Dogs with liver disease must eat small meals of complex carbohydrates frequently throughout the day in order to get better. They should avoid meat and instead get their protein from milk or soy products. Vitamin A and copper levels must be kept low.

Pancreatitis: Pancreatitis requires a low-fat diet.

Congestive heart failure: Dogs with heart failure require a low-sodium diet in order to lower their blood pressure. This will help reduce the accumulation of fluid in the lungs or abdomen.

Kidney disease: Diets for kidney disease should have moderate quantities of high quality protein, and low phosphorus and sodium levels.

waistline, both when viewed from above and from the side.

Overweight: If your Eskie is fat, do not allow her to continue overeating. Try a less fattening food or feed less of your current food; make sure family members aren't sneaking her tidbits. If your Eskie remains overweight, seek your veterinarian's advice. Obese Eskies miss out on a lot of fun in life, and are prone to joint injuries and a shortened life span.

Finicky eaters: Finicky eaters are another special challenge. Many picky eaters are

created when their owners begin to spice up their food with especially tasty treats. The dog then refuses to eat unless the preferred treat is offered, and finally learns that if they refuse to eat even that proffered treat, another even tastier enticement will be offered. Give your Eskie a good, tasty meal, but don't succumb to Eskie blackmail or you may be a slave to your dog's gastronomical whims for years to come. Fortunately, most Eskies are far too gluttonous to exhibit the self-control necessary for such a ruse.

GROOMING YOUR AMERICAN ESKIMO DOG

The upkeep of an Eskimo dog requires a little grooming often, rather than a lot of grooming seldom.

That white powder-puff coat is no doubt one of the Eskie's most undeniable charms. The upkeep of such a crowning glory may at first seem intimidating, but a short grooming session once or twice a week will usually suffice to keep both you and your Eskie proud.

Starting Early

You may wish to use a grooming table, but it is equally effective to have the dog lie on a towel while being brushed. Many dogs and owners look forward to such grooming sessions as a relaxing time of bonding. Of course, if your Eskie is screaming and kicking and you're grabbing and pulling you will probably achieve relatively little relaxation or bonding from the experience. Start right, by grooming your puppy before he's had time to develop any tangles, so brushing feels even better than petting to him. Make a

Think white!

routine of spending just a few minutes every day grooming. Keeping sessions short, fun, and rewarding. In the puppy, you need not follow the full grooming routine; remember, although you certainly want to prevent the formation of any tangles, your most important long-term goal now is training the pup to be cooperative.

Coat Disasters

You may be faced with some coat disasters on occasion.

✔ Chewing gum can be eased out by first applying ice.

✔ Pine tar can be loosened with hair spray; other tar can be worked out with vegetable oil followed by dishwashing detergent.

✔ Tight mats and burrs can be helped by soaking for an hour in tangle remover or vegetable oil.

✔ Skunk odor may be helped by a solution of one pint 3% hydrogen peroxide, 2/3 cup baking soda, and one teaspoon liquid soap.

Keeping red stains off your Eskie may take some work, but can be done.

Stains

White dogs can get red stains from exposure to their own saliva or tears. If your Eskie has tearstains below the eyes or reddened fur around the lips, your first job is to find out why.

Tearstains: The eyes may be producing excessive tears because of irritation, or the eyes may not be draining away the tears normally. Your veterinarian can tell with a simple test. Some dogs, especially toy dogs, tend to not drain tears adequately, and as a result are plagued by tearstains. Some oral antibiotics can temporarily change the chemical composition of the tears and stop them from staining, but the staining resumes when the dog stops taking the drugs. Your best bet is to wipe away the tears as often as possible, and place a water-resistant barrier such as petroleum jelly beneath the eye.

Lips: Staining around the lips may indicate that your dog is licking his lips too often, which can sometimes signal dental problems. Once again, a trip to the veterinarian is the first step.

Toes: Staining around the toes can result when dogs lick their feet, or it can come from feet that are always wet between the toes. If the dog is licking, it could signal an allergy, and once again, it's time for a veterinary check. If they're just wet, the obvious answer is to keep them dry. Cornstarch may help dry them up.

Red stains: You can remove red stains with a mixture of equal parts hydrogen peroxide, cornstarch, and milk of magnesia. Apply with a toothbrush, being extremely careful to keep it away from the eyes, as hydrogen peroxide can harm the eyes. Allow it to dry, then hold the eye shut and use a toothbrush to brush the residue away. You may have to repeat this several times.

Coat Trimming

The Eskie is a natural breed, meaning trimming the coat is neither necessary nor desired. For show purposes, some exhibitors tidy up the feet and hocks.

Feet: You can tidy up the feet by carefully trimming the shaggy hairs so that the foot appears small, neat, and compact. Brush the hair on the rear of the hock upward and trim the ragged edges parallel to the bone. Even if you are not trying to create a show dog look, trimmed feet track in less mud.

Whiskers: The American Eskimo Dog is an exception to the general rule that show dogs must have their whiskers trimmed. It is a credit to the fanciers of this breed that they demand these important sensory organs remain intact on their dogs whether at home or in the ring.

Nail Trimming

Trimming and fluffing is optional for everyday life, but nail trimming is not. Begin by handling the feet and nails daily, and then "tipping" the ends of your puppy's nails every week, taking special care not to cut the "quick" (the central core of blood vessels and nerve endings). In puppies or toys, a scissors-type clipper may be easier, whereas in minis or standards, a guillotine nail clipper is usually preferable.

Rear nails first: The nails are softer after a bath. Most dogs are less sensitive about having their rear nails done, so do these first. Remember the pictures of the village blacksmith shoe-

It's often easier to clip nails by holding the foot and looking at its underside, where you can see the hollow end of the nail. Cut the hollow part off.

= T I P =

Dewclaws

If your dog has dewclaws, do not neglect trimming them, as well, because left untrimmed they can get caught on things more easily or actually loop around and grow into the dog's leg.

---

ing a horse? Hold your dog's feet behind it, so that you are looking at the bottoms of the toenails. You will see a solid core culminating in a hollowed nail. Cut the tip up to the core, but not beyond. One advantage of light-colored nails is that you can see the pink inner core of blood vessels, so this is another clue about where to avoid cutting.

Front nails: Repeat the procedure with the front nails, which tend to grow longer than the rear. Again, if you hold the feet curled behind the leg, dogs seem to accept it better, perhaps because they can't see what you are doing.

Well-groomed Eskies seem to take pride in their appearance.

Tips: Don't be surprised if your Eskie, nonetheless, does everything in his power to convince the neighborhood that you are amputating his toes. Speak soothingly, be firm, but don't let a battle ensue. If you must compromise just cut the very tip off and come back later for a shorter cut. Give a reward for good behavior, perhaps after each nail.

Bleeding

On occasion you will slip up and cause the nail to bleed. This is best stopped by styptic powder, but if this is not available, dip the nail in flour or hold it to a wet teabag. Of course your Eskie will take this opportunity to convince you and everyone who will listen that you have, indeed, committed a heinous crime of animal abuse, but the truth is you would be far more abusive to let his nails grow unchecked. When you can hear the pitter-patter of clicking nails, that means that with every step the nails are hitting the floor, and when this happens the

bones of the foot are spread, causing discomfort and eventually splayed feet and lameness.

Skin and Coat Problems

A healthy coat depends on healthy skin. Skin allergies, parasites, and infections can make your dog uncomfortable and unhealthy.

Allergies

Scratching, chewing, rubbing, and licking may be signs of allergies, perhaps in response to inhaled allergens, things they come in contact with, foods, or fleas. Unlike humans, where hay fever and other inhaled allergens typically cause sneezing, in dogs they more often cause itching. Food, too, can cause allergies. Signs of allergies are typically reddened itchy skin, particularly around the ears, eyes, feet, forelegs, armpits, and abdomen. The dog may scratch and lick, and rub her torso or rear on furniture or rugs.

A beautiful coat depends on a healthy skin.

The most common inhaled allergens are dander, pollen, dust, and mold. They are often seasonal. Allergens can be isolated with a skin test in which small amounts of allergen extracts are injected under the skin. Each injection site is then monitored for reactions. Besides avoiding allergens, some treatments are available. Treatment includes antihistamines, glucocorticoids, and hyposensitization.

FAD: The most common allergy among all dogs is flea allergy dermatitis (FAD), which is an allergic reaction to the saliva that a flea injects under the skin whenever it feeds. Not only does it cause intense itching in that area, but all over the dog, especially around the rump, legs, and paws. Even a single flea bite can cause severe reactions in allergic dogs.

Hot Spots

A hot spot, technically known as pyrotraumatic dermatitis, is an area of skin that is irritated, perhaps by a flea bite, so that the dog scratches or chews the area. It quickly becomes enlarged, infected, and painful. Treat by clipping away hair and cleansing the area with surgical soap. Some people find that washing with Listerine gives good results. Apply an antibiotic cream, or better, an antibiotic powder. Prevent the dog from further chewing and scratching.

Hair Loss

In some cases, hair is lost without the dog itching. Demodectic mange, thyroid deficiency,

estrogen excess, ringworm, and seborrhea are all possibilities that your veterinarian can diagnose.

Blisters

Blisters and brown crust on the stomach of your Eskimo puppy indicate puppy impetigo. Clean the area twice daily with dilute hydrogen peroxide or surgical soap, and treat with a topical antibiotic.

Lumps

Most bumps and lumps are not cause for concern, but because there is always a possibility of cancer, they should be examined by your veterinarian. This is especially true of a sore that does not heal, or any pigmented lump that begins to grow or bleed.

Brushing

✔ Begin brushing the face, moving rearward on one side and then the other. If the dog becomes restless, move to another area, returning to the trouble spot later.

✔ Use a pin brush to brush the hair in layers so that it is brushed down to the skin.

✔ As your finishing touch, comb all the long hair toward the head, so the hair stands away from the body.

Matting: Mats can form behind the ears or the elbows, especially during shedding season or when it is oily or dirty. Never wash a matted coat; the mat will only become tighter.

Try to split a mat with your fingers, starting near the skin and pulling it in half longitudinally. Hold the hair between

Brush the coat against the direction of growth to make it stand off the body. Misting the coat with water before brushing will decrease static and breakage.

the mat and the skin to avoid pain. Stubborn mats may require splitting with a rake, or as a last resort, cut out with scissors. Even with scissors, split the mat into halves. To avoid accidentally cutting the skin, push a fine comb between mat and skin before you start.

Shedding

An Eskimo Dog shedding its coat can best be compared to a field of dandelion puffs in a hurricane.

✔ Use a slicker brush to remove loose hair.

✔ A flat-based slicker is best for the medium-length Eskie coat.

✔ Shedding can be further hastened by bathing, which loosens the hair follicles.

✔ If you are trying to keep as much coat as possible on your Eskie for as long as possible, do not bathe him when he begins shedding.

Controlling shedding: Shedding is controlled not by exposure to warmer temperatures, but by exposure to longer periods of light. This is why indoor dogs, exposed to artificial light, tend to shed somewhat all year. Shedding is also hormonally controlled in females, so that a shedding period follows each season or a litter.

Among the grooming tools you will need are (clockwise from bottom left) a slicker brush, pin brush, comb, mat rake, and scissors.

Bathing

Shampoo: You will get better results with a shampoo made for dogs. Dog skin has a pH of 7.5, whereas human skin has a pH of 5.5; thus, bathing in a shampoo for humans can lead to scaling and irritation. That's not to say that you can't use human shampoo in a pinch, but if your Eskie has any skin problems, be careful about what shampoo you use.

Many shampoos claim to make white coats whiter; the newer ones without bluing are probably easier on the skin. Most shampoos will kill fleas even if not especially formulated as a flea shampoo, but none has any residual killing action on fleas. There is a variety of therapeutic shampoos for use with skin problems.

✔ Dry scaly skin is treated with moisturizing shampoos.

✔ Excessive scale and dandruff are treated with antiseborrheic shampoos (but be careful here: the tar or selenium sulfide shampoos commonly used for this can stain).

✔ Damaged skin is treated with antimicrobials (again, iodine-based shampoos can stain).

✔ Itchy skin is treated with antipruritics (often oatmeal-based).

✔ Benzoyl peroxide (2.5 to 3 percent), available at your pharmacy, is a good antiseborrhea/antimicrobial shampoo and safe for white coats.

Note: Always have one of the shampoos that requires no water or rinsing. These are wonderful for puppies, emergencies, and last minute cleanups.

Bath Techniques

Even the most devoted of owners seldom look forward to bathtime. Invariably the owner ends up at least as wet as the dog, and certainly in no better mood. In fact, at least the dog is happy when he gets out of the tub; the owner is left to clean up what appears to be major flood damage.

Unfortunately, most owners bring this scenario on themselves through improper early bath training. The secret is to give tiny baths, so tiny the puppy doesn't get scared or tired. Rinse (don't even wash) one leg today, the back tomorrow, and so on. Be firm, soothing, and playful. A bath should be a pleasurable experience for both of you.

Full bath: Once you have worked up to a full-scale bath, begin with a thorough brushing to remove tangles and distribute oils; then wet your dog down, working forward. Use water that would be comfortable for you to bathe in, and be sure to monitor any temperature changes. Beware that a fractious Eskie could inadvertently

Rinse your Eskie thoroughly, working from the head back to the tail.

hit a faucet knob and be scalded. As long as you keep one hand on your dog's neck or ear, he is less likely to splatter you.

Once your Eskie's coat is soaked, work in the shampoo (it will go farther and be easier to apply if you first dilute it with warm water). Pay special attention to the oily area around the ear base, but avoid getting water in the dog's ears (try plugging with cotton). Rinse thoroughly, this time working from the head back.

Drying: Your Eskie will love being towel dried, but be sure not to rub to the point of creating tangles; for special occasions, blow dry while brushing the hair backward. Again, you must accustom your dog to a drier gradually, and always keep your hand where you are drying; once your hand gets uncomfortably hot, you know the dog's skin must also be uncomfortable.

Try to split matted hair with your fingers, starting near the skin and pulling it apart into sections.

A long life depends on good genes, good luck, and good care. You and your veterinarian are the ones responsible for your Eskie's good care.

Choosing Your Veterinarian

Choose a veterinarian with as much care as you would your own doctor. Consider availability, facilities, and ability to communicate. Your rapport with your veterinarian is very important. Your veterinarian should listen to your observations, and should explain to you exactly what is happening with your Eskie. Ask questions, be sure you understand directions for medications before leaving the office, and be sure that you follow them once you get home.

When you take your Eskie to the veterinary clinic, restrain your dog on a leash and do not allow her to mingle with the other patients that may be sick or frightened. Your veterinarian will be appreciative if your Eskie is clean and under control during her examination.

Keep your Eskie smiling by ensuring her good health.

Emergencies

Emergencies don't always occur during office hours. Know the phone number and location of the emergency veterinarian in your area. Drive carefully and smoothly, or have someone else drive while you tend to your dog.

Deciding whether or not you have an emergency can be difficult. When in doubt, call the veterinarian or emergency clinic. The following situations are all *life-threatening emergencies*. For all cases, administer the first aid treatment outlined and seek the nearest veterinary help *immediately*. Call the clinic first so that they can be prepared for your dog when you arrive.

Shock

Signs: Very pale gums, weakness, unresponsiveness, faint pulse, shivering.

Treatment: Keep the dog warm and calm; control any bleeding; check breathing, pulse, and consciousness and treat these problems if needed.

═══ TIP ═══

General Instructions

✔ Make sure breathing passages are open. Loosen the collar and check the mouth and throat.

✔ Be calm and reassuring.

✔ Move the dog as little and as gently as possible.

✔ If the dog is in pain, she may bite. Apply a makeshift muzzle with a bandage, belt, or tape. Do not muzzle if breathing difficulties are present.

Heatstroke

Signs: Rapid loud breathing, abundant thick saliva, bright red mucous membranes, and high rectal temperature. Later signs include unsteadiness, diarrhea, and coma.

Treatment: Wet the dog down and place her in front of a fan. If this isn't possible, immerse her in cold water. Don't plunge her in ice water, because that constricts the peripheral blood vessels so much that they can't cool the blood as well. Offer water to drink.

You must lower your dog's body temperature quickly, but don't let the temperature go below 100°F (37.8°C). Stop cooling when the rectal temperature reaches 103°F (39.4°C) because it will continue to fall.

Even when the temperature is back to normal your Eskie is still in danger and still needs veterinary attention. It will take several days for your dog to recover, during which he should not be allowed to exert herself.

Breathing Difficulties

Signs: Gasping with head extended, anxiety, weakness; advances to loss of consciousness, bluish tongue (exception: carbon monoxide poisoning causes bright red tongue).

Treatment: If not breathing, give mouth-to-nose respiration:

1. Open the dog's mouth; clear passage of secretions and foreign bodies.

2. Pull the dog's tongue forward; close the dog's mouth; seal the dog's lips with your hand.

3. Seal your mouth over the dog's nose; blow into the dog's nose for three seconds, then release.

4. Continue until the dog breathes on her own.

If due to drowning, turn the dog upside down, holding her by the hind legs, so that water can run out of her mouth. Then administer mouth-to-nose respiration, with the dog's head positioned lower than her lungs.

Bloat or Gastric Torsion

Signs: Restlessness, distended abdomen, unproductive attempts to vomit.

Treatment: Get to the nearest veterinarian *at once*. This is a life-threatening emergency—delay can cause irreversible damage and death. Treat for shock en route and monitor breathing.

Poisoning

Signs: Vomiting, depression, and convulsions, depending on type of poison. When in doubt, call your veterinarian or the ASPCA Animal Poison Control Center at (888) 426-4435.

Treatment: If the poison was ingested in the past two hours, and if it's not an acid, alkali, petroleum product, solvent, or tranquilizer, you may be advised to induce vomiting by giving hydrogen peroxide or dry mustard mixed 1:1

with water. Ipecac syrup is not recommended for this purpose in dogs. In other cases you may be advised to dilute the poison by giving milk or vegetable oil. Activated charcoal can adsorb many toxins. Poisons act in different ways, so it's important to have the label of any suspected poisons available.

✔ Ethylene glycol-based antifreeze is a dog killer. Even tiny amounts cause irreversible kidney damage, and the prognosis is poor once symptoms appear. Get emergency help if you suspect your dog drank antifreeze.

✔ Rodent poisons are either warfarin-based, which cause uncontrolled internal bleeding, or cholecalciferol-based, which cause kidney failure.

✔ Bird and squirrel poisons are usually strychnine-based, which cause neurological malfunction.

✔ Insect poisons, weed killers, and wood preservatives may be arsenic-based and cause kidney failure.

✔ Flea, tick, and internal parasite poisons may contain organophosphates, which can cause neurological symptoms.

✔ Iron-based rose fertilizers can cause kidney and liver failure.

Convulsions

Signs: Drooling, stiffness, muscle spasms.

Treatment: Prevent the dog from injuring herself on the furniture or stairs. Remove other dogs from the area. Treat for shock. Contact your veterinarian.

Open Wounds

Signs: Consider wounds to be an emergency if there is profuse bleeding, if extremely deep, if open to chest cavity, abdominal cavity, or head.

Lethargy is a common sign of illness.

Treatment: Control massive bleeding first. Cover the wound with a clean dressing and apply pressure; apply more dressings over the others until bleeding stops. Also, elevate the wound site, and apply a cold pack to the site.

If an extremity, apply pressure to the closest pressure point as follows:

✔ For a front leg: inside of the front leg just above the elbow.

✔ For a rear leg: inside of the thigh where the femoral artery crosses the thigh bone.

✔ For the tail: underside of the tail close to where it joins the body.

Use a tourniquet only in life-threatening situations and when all other attempts have failed. Check for signs of shock.

Sucking chest wounds: Place a sheet of plastic or other nonporous material over the hole and bandage it to make an airtight seal.

Abdominal wounds: Place a warm, wet, sterile dressing over any protruding internal organs; cover with a bandage or towel. Do not attempt to push organs back into the dog.

Head wounds: Apply gentle pressure to control bleeding. Monitor for loss of consciousness or shock and treat accordingly.

Deep Burns

Signs: Charred or pearly white skin; deeper layers of tissue exposed.

Treatment: Cool burned area with cool packs, towels soaked in ice water, or by immersing in cold water. If over 50 percent of the dog is burned, do not immerse as this increases the likelihood of shock. Cover with a clean bandage or towel to avoid contamination. Do not apply pressure; do not apply ointments. Monitor for shock.

Electrical Shock

Signs: Collapse, burns inside mouth.

Treatment: Before touching the dog, disconnect the plug or cut power. If that cannot be done immediately, use a wooden pencil, spoon, or broom handle to knock the cord away from the dog. Keep the dog warm and treat for shock. Monitor breathing and heartbeat.

The above list is by no means a complete catalog of emergency situations. Situations not described can usually be treated with the same first aid as for humans. You should maintain a first aid/medical kit for your Eskie, which should contain at least: rectal thermometer, scissors, tweezers, sterile gauze dressings, self-adhesive bandage, instant cold compress, antidiarrhea medication, ophthalmic ointment, soap, antiseptic skin ointment, hydrogen peroxide, first aid instructions, and veterinarian and emergency clinic numbers.

Preventive Medicine

The best preventive medicine is that which prevents accidents: a well-trained dog in a well-fenced yard or on a leash, and a properly Eskie-proofed home. Other preventive steps must be taken to avoid diseases and parasites, however.

External Parasites

Fleas: These bloodsuckers can ruin your Eskie's beautiful coat, make her life miserable, and in some cases even lead to anemia and death. They can be found anywhere on the dog, but prefer the underside and around the tail base. They leave behind a black pepperlike substance (actually flea feces), which turns red upon getting wet. Some Eskies develop an allergic reaction to the saliva of the flea; one bite can cause them to itch and chew for days. Flea allergies are typically characterized by loss of coat and little red bumps around the lower back and tail base.

Recent advances in flea control have finally put fleas on the run. These products have a higher initial purchase price but are cheaper in the long run because they work and they need only be reapplied every few months. Most of these products are available only from your veterinarian, although some discount products try to sound like they work the same. Look for a product with one of the following ingredients:

✔ Imidacloprid: a self-distributing liquid that kills fleas within a day and continues for a month. It can withstand water, but not repeated bathing.

✔ Fipronil: a spray or self-distributing liquid that collects in the hair follicles and wicks out over time. It kills fleas for up to three months and ticks for a shorter time, and is resistant to bathing.

✔ Selamectin: a self-distributing liquid that kills fleas for one month. It also kills ear mites and several internal parasites, and acts as a heartworm preventive.

✔ Nytenpyram: oral medication that starts killing fleas in 20 minutes; all fleas are killed in four hours. It has almost no residual activity, so it's mostly for a quick fix of heavily infested dogs.

✔ Lufenuron, methoprene, or fenoxycarb: chemicals that render any fleas that bite the dog sterile.

Note: Most over-the-counter products are permethrin based, which isn't resistant to water and doesn't kill fleas for long. Flea populations can easily become resistant to it. In fact, fleas can become resistant to any treatment, so the best strategy is to change products frequently and to include the use of both a flea killer and a flea sterilizer.

Ticks: Ticks are also a pesky disease-carrying pest. Rocky Mountain spotted fever, Lyme disease, and, most commonly, "tick fever" (erhlichiosis) are potentially fatal diseases carried by ticks. Ticks most often attach around the ears and neck area, but may also be found hiding between your Eskie's toes. Use a tissue or tweezers to remove ticks, because some diseases can be transmitted to humans. Kill the tick first with alcohol, if desired. Then pull slowly and steadily, trying not to leave the head in the dog. If the head is left in, keep an eye on the area to make sure an infection does not result. Do not attempt to burn the tick out; you may set fire to your Eskie!

Ear mites: Ear mites are highly communicable and often found in puppies. Affected dogs will shake their head, scratch their ears, and carry their head sideways. There is a dark waxy buildup in the ear canal, usually of both ears. If you place some of this wax on a piece of dark paper, and have very good eyes, you may be able to see tiny white moving specks. These are the culprits. Although there are over-the-counter ear mite preparations, they can cause worse irritation. Therefore, ear mites should be diagnosed and treated by your veterinarian. Treatment may include drug therapy, eardrops, whole-body dips, and washing of bedding. Other household pets may also need treatment.

Mange mites: Dogs are prone to two very different forms of mange. Sarcoptic mange is highly contagious to dogs and humans. Characterized by intense itching and often scaling of the ear tips, it is easily treated with dips. Demodectic mange is not contagious and does not itch, but can be difficult to cure. It tends to run in families, and is characterized by a moth-eaten

It's a jungle out there!

appearance, often on the face or feet. Advanced cases lead to serious secondary staphylococcal infections. Some localized forms may go away on their own, but more widespread cases will need a special dip regime prescribed by your veterinarian. Systemic drug therapies are also available.

Dental Care

At around four to five months of age, your Eskie puppy will begin to shed her baby teeth and show off new permanent teeth. Sometimes baby teeth, especially the canines, are not shed, so that the permanent tooth grows in beside the baby tooth. If this condition persists for more than a couple of days, consult your veterinarian. Retained baby teeth can cause misalignment of adult teeth. Check the way your puppy's teeth match up; in a correct bite, the bottom incisors should touch the back of the top incisors when the mouth is closed. Deviations from this can cause chewing problems and discomfort.

Without brushing, plaque and tartar spread rootward causing irreversible periodontal disease with tissue, bone, and tooth loss. The bacteria gain an inlet to the bloodstream, where they can cause kidney and heart valve infections.

Brushing is the best way to keep your Eskie's teeth healthy. But if you find it impossible, the next best things are special dog foods, chews, and toys designed to inhibit tartar. Hard crunchy foods can help, but they won't take the place of brushing. If tartar accumulates, your Eskie may need a thorough cleaning under anesthesia. You wouldn't think of going days, weeks, months, or even years without brushing your teeth. Why would you expect your dog to?

Hereditary Concerns

Like every breed of dog, the American Eskimo Dog has its own smattering of disorders in its gene pool. Responsible breeders screen for these disorders. In some cases, the affected dog is best neutered or spayed, whereas in others, the dog has a low grade of the disorder and enough other superior traits that it's worth breeding the dog to another dog that does not have the disorder. The Eskie's main hereditary disorders are progressive retinal atrophy, hip dysplasia, and patellar luxation.

Progressive Retinal Atrophy

The American Eskimo Dog's most significant hereditary problem is a form of eye disease known as Progressive Retinal Atrophy (PRA). Several types of PRA exist in dogs; the type that Eskies have is progressive rod-cone degeneration, or prcd-PRA. It is a recessively inherited condition, meaning that an affected dog must inherent a copy of the mutant gene from both parents. A dog with only one such copy is a carrier and will be unaffected.

Results: PRA causes irreversible blindness; no treatment for it exists. It affects the eye's rods and cones, the cells of the retina that transmit light into nerve impulses. Rods, which are more sensitive to dim light, are affected first, so dogs initially have difficulty finding their way in dim light. This is especially apparent in unfamiliar or awkward places. The condition slowly worsens until the dog is essentially night-blind. Meanwhile the cones, too, begin to deteriorate. Cones are responsible for detail, color, and bright light vision, so these abilities begin to fade. The dog's pupils dilate in an effort to allow more light in, and owners may notice increased "eye shine" from the pupils.

Progression: Affected Eskies are typically diagnosed at around four to six years of age, which is later than in most other breeds with *prcd*-PRA. The disease progresses slowly in Eskies, so a diagnosis doesn't necessarily mean a dog will be totally blind by old age. PRA isn't painful, and most dogs adjust to their gradually dimming world. A blind dog can live a full and happy life, especially if you take care to not place surprises in their path.
✔ Keep furniture in the same place.
✔ Keep the floor tidy.
✔ Provide scent or auditory beacons around the house and yard.
✔ Make pathways from carpet runners, stone, or other materials so the dog can easily tell when he's on the right path simply by how it feels underfoot.

Diagnosis: PRA can be diagnosed by examining the dog's eyes through an ophthalmoscope or by examining the eyes' electrical response to

The eyes are the windows to the soul—keep them clear and healthy.

light by means of an electroretinogram. These tests are painless and neither requires anesthesia, but they should be performed by a veterinary ophthalmologist (visit *www.acvo.org* for a list of veterinary ophthalmologists in your area). Results can be listed with the Canine Eye Registration Foundation (CERF; see contact information on page 92). Approximately 9 percent of Eskies with CERF data have signs of PRA, indicating that this is a significant concern in the breed.

DNA test: In 2004 a DNA test became available to detect the probable presence of the gene for *prcd*-PRA in American Eskimo Dogs. This test, available through Optigen (*www.optigen.com*), is a marker test, which means it detects the presence of a DNA sequence that is almost always inherited along with the mutated *prcd*-PRA gene because it is very close to it on the chromosome. Because this test detects a DNA marker, rather than the actual mutated gene, there is a small chance (at most, 0.5 percent) that on rare occasions it will be wrong. The test classifies Eskies into three risk groups:

1. Pattern A: "Homozygous normal." These dogs probably have two normal gene copies. They are not expected to develop or pass on *prcd*-PRA.

━━━ TIP ━━━

Deciphering an OFA Number

An OFA number carries a lot of information. Using a hypothetical number of **AE-1000G24M-PI**, here's how it breaks down:

✔ **AE** identifies the breed as American Eskimo.

✔ **1000** indicates this is the 1000th Eskie to receive an OFA number.

✔ **G** is the rating, in this case "good." E would indicate Excellent and F would indicate Fair.

✔ **24** is the dog's age in months at the time it was radiographed.

✔ **M** is the dog's sex, in this case male. F would indicate female.

✔ **PI** indicates the dog is permanently identified with a tattoo or microchip. NOPI would indicate the dog had no such permanent identification.

2. Pattern B: "Heterozygous carrier." These dogs probably have one normal and one mutant *prcd* gene. They are not expected to develop *prcd*-PRA, but they can pass it on if bred.

3. Pattern C: "Homozygous affected." These dogs will probably develop *prcd*-PRA, and will pass it on if bred.

Any potential breeding stock should have a DNA test for prcd-PRA. Pattern A dogs can be bred to Pattern A, B, or C dogs without fear of producing affected puppies. Pattern B or Pattern C dogs should be bred only to Pattern A dogs, otherwise they may produce affected puppies. The goal at this time is to avoid producing affected puppies.

Other retinal diseases: Making sure that at least one parent is a Pattern A should negate the chance of producing *prcd*-PRA affected dogs, but it doesn't negate the chance of producing dogs with other, less common, retinal diseases. Eskies can also develop a nonhereditary retinal disease called multifocal retinopathy, which can lead to patches of retinal atrophy in one or both eyes. Don't assume that an Eskie with visual problems has *prcd*-PRA; always have such a dog checked by a veterinary ophthalmologist, and have a DNA test as well. It could be a totally different problem, perhaps one that is treatable.

Hip Dysplasia

Like many breeds, Eskies are also susceptible to hip dysplasia, a hereditary disorder that affects how the ball of the femur (thighbone) nests in the socket of the pelvic bone. The fit is affected both by the depth and shape of the socket as well as the laxity of the joint. When the dog puts pressure on the joint by walking or running, the ball slips in and out of the socket. Each time it does this, it wears down the socket rim and gradually worsens the situation, which is one reason hip dysplasia gets worse with time.

Hip radiographs (X rays) can diagnose hip dysplasia before outward signs are noticeable. Your veterinarian can take the radiographs and send them to the Orthopedic Foundation for Animals (OFA) for reading and certification. Dogs rated as having normal hips (which includes ratings of excellent, good, and fair) receive OFA numbers. Dogs considered dysplastic have ratings of mild, moderate, and severe. Dogs with borderline ratings should be rechecked in six to eight months.

PennHip: OFA numbers are only issued based on radiographs taken after the dog is 24 months

DNA tests can determine which puppies are likely to develop prcd-PRA, *which are carriers, and which are clear.*

old, although OFA will issue preliminary ratings for younger dogs. The Pennsylvania Hip Improvement Program (PennHip), which uses a slightly different technique based on objective measures of joint laxity, issues ratings at a much younger age. Their procedure must be preformed by a PennHip-approved veterinarian.

OFA records show that about 9 percent of all Eskies evaluated by them are considered dysplastic, with only 7 percent rated Excellent. The trend appears to be toward better hips, however, perhaps because of careful breeding practices. Although hip dysplasia is more common in larger dog breeds, Eskies of all sizes have been known to be affected, and it doesn't seem that any one size is affected more than another.

Treatment: Mild hip dysplasia may not need specific treatment, but more severe cases may require surgery. In these cases the sooner the surgery is done, the better the results. In such dogs a triple pelvic osteotomy, in which the orientation of the hip socket is changed so the femur head fits more snugly, may be the best option. Older dogs or dogs with more advanced dysplasia may be better candidates for total hip replacement, in which the socket is replaced with a Teflon cup and the femur head with a metallic ball. Simply removing the hip altogether is less expensive and may prove satisfactory for an older, more sedate dog, especially a smaller Eskie, but not for a large or active one.

Hip dysplasia is considered hereditary, but not in a simple dominant versus recessive fashion. It is probably the result of the interplay of several genes, each adding its effect. When considering such polygenic traits, it's as important to consider the hip status of siblings of dogs in a pedi-

TIP

Pain

Of course, dogs can feel pain. But because a dog may not be able to express its condition, you must be alert to changes in your dog's demeanor. A stiff gait, a reluctance to get up, irritability, dilated pupils, whining, or limping are all indications of pain. Some dogs are more stoic than others, so you must learn to read your individual dog.

gree as well as its direct ancestors. Feeding is also a consideration; feeding large breeds puppy foods that encourage rapid growth can make a dog that is predisposed to hip dysplasia more likely to develop it. Talk to your veterinarian about the optimal puppy food for your Eskie, especially if she comes from a background of dogs with hip dysplasia.

Patellar Luxation

The dog's knee, or stifle, is the joint connecting the femur (thigh) bone to the tibia and fibula. The knee joint contains three small bones, including the patella, or kneecap. When the knee flexes, the patella normally glides along the trochlear groove of the femur, held within the groove by the quadriceps muscle and joint capsule. In some Eskies the groove is too shallow, or the quadriceps' rotational pull is too strong, allowing the patella to ride over the groove's ridge when the knee is flexed. Only straightening the knee will cause the patella to go back into place. Affected dogs will often take several steps with a hind leg held straight toward the front until the patella pops back into place. It may hurt when it does, so the dog may yelp. In more severe cases, the luxated patella can't pop back on its own. Each time it goes in and out of the groove it wears down the groove's edge, which in turn can cause arthritic changes.

Treatment depends on severity:

✔ For Grade 1, in which the patella seldom pops out of place on its own, and the dog may hold her leg up for a step or two, no treatment is suggested.

✔ For Grade 2, in which the dog often holds her leg up when walking or running, and in which the patella may not pop back in on its own, treatment is seldom suggested.

✔ For Grade 3, in which the dog seldom uses the affected leg, and the patella is permanently out of position, surgery may be suggested.

✔ For Grade 4, in which the dog never uses the affected leg and the patella can't be replaced even manually, surgery is usually suggested.

Patellar luxation is thought to have a strong hereditary basis, probably, like hip dysplasia, inherited in a polygenic fashion. The OFA maintains a registry of Eskies that have been checked for patellar luxation. At this writing about 7 percent of OFA-registered Eskies had abnormal patellas. Patellar luxation is generally more common in small and toy dog breeds. No data have been collected comparing its incidence in various Eskie sizes; it occurs in all sizes, but some breeders feel it is more common in smaller Eskies.

Signs and Sickness

It's not easy to know when your Eskie needs medical attention. When in doubt, have her checked out. Meanwhile, consider these questions.

Are her gums pink? If you think your Eskie is sick, one of the first things to check is her gum color. Gums should be a deep pink, and if you press with your thumb, they should return to pink within two seconds after lifting your thumb (a longer time suggests a circulatory problem). Very pale gums may indicate anemia, shock, or poor circulation. Bluish gums or tongue can mean a life-threatening lack of oxygen. Bright red gums may indicate overheating or carbon monoxide poisoning, and yellow gums jaundice. Tiny red splotches may indicate a blood-clotting problem. Tooth and gum problems will often cause bad breath and pain.

Is she acting different than usual? Sick dogs are often lethargic. They may lie quietly in a curled position, often in an out-of-the-way place. Possible causes include fever, anemia, circulatory problems, nausea, poisoning, sudden vision loss, chronic illness, or pain. Irritability, restlessness, hiding, clawing, panting, and trembling may indicate pain. Dogs with abdominal pain often stretch and bow.

A dog with breathing difficulties will often refuse to lie down or, if she does, will keep her head raised. Confusion, head-pressing, or seizures may indicate neurological problems. Any sudden behavior change warrants a veterinary examination.

Is she eating less than usual? Loss of appetite is most often associated with illness, although increased appetite may accompany some endocrine disorders. A slight decrease in appetite is expected in warm weather, but not so much that she loses weight. If your dog refuses her meal for more than one or two meals, or if she has a gradual decline in her interest in food and is losing weight, a thorough veterinary exam is needed.

TIP

Temperature and Pulse

To take your dog's temperature, lubricate a rectal thermometer and insert it about 2 inches (5 cm) into the dog's anus, leaving it there for about a minute. Normal is from 101 to 102°F (38.3–38.9°C). If the temperature is

✔ 103°F (39.4°C) or above, call your veterinarian for advice. This is not usually an emergency.

✔ 105°F (41°C) or above, go to your veterinarian. This is probably an emergency; 106°F (41.1°C) or above is dangerous. Try to cool your dog.

✔ 98°F (36.7°C) or below, call your veterinarian for advice. Try to warm your dog.

✔ 96°F (35.6°C) or below, go to your veterinarian. Treat for hypothermia on the way by warming your dog.

To check the pulse, cup your hand around the top of your dog's rear leg so your fingers are near the top, almost where the leg joins the body. Feel for the pulse in the femoral artery. Normal adult Eskie pulse rate is 70 to 120 beats per minute.

Check hydration by touching the gums, which should be slick, not sticky, or by lifting the skin on the back and letting it go. It should snap back into place quickly, not remain tented. Sticky gums and tented skin indicate dehydration. If your dog has been vomiting or has diarrhea, she may instantly lose any water you give her, in which case your veterinarian may need to give your dog fluids under the skin, or better, in a vein.

Is she drinking or urinating more than usual? Increased thirst, usually with increased urination, may indicate kidney disease or diabetes. A sudden and frequent urge to urinate, usually in small amounts and often accompanied by signs of pain, may indicate a urinary tract infection. Painful urination, straining to urinate, or blood in the urine may indicate urinary stones. Inability to urinate is a life-threatening emergency.

Is she vomiting? Vomiting after eating grass is not unusual and is seldom a cause for concern, but repeated vomiting can signal internal parasites, poisoning, blockage, or a host of problems. Consult your veterinarian immediately if your dog vomits feceslike matter (which could indicate an intestinal blockage) or blood (which may resemble coffee grounds), has accompanying fever or pain, or if the vomiting lasts more than a few hours.

Does she have diarrhea? Diarrhea can result from nervousness, a change in diet or water, food sensitivities, intestinal parasites, infections, poisoning, or many illnesses. It's not uncommon for dogs to have blood in their diarrhea, but diarrhea with lots of blood or accompanied by vomiting, fever, or other symptoms of illness warrants a call to the veterinarian. Bright red blood indicates a source lower in the digestive tract, while dark black tarry stools indicate a source higher in the digestive tract.

Is she coughing? Coughing can be caused by foreign bodies, tracheal collapse, tumors, kennel cough, and heart disease, among other causes. Congestive heart failure causes coughing and breathing difficulties mainly after exercise and at night and early morning. Kennel cough is a communicable airborne disease caused by several infectious agents. It is characterized by a gagging or honking cough, often a week after being around infected dogs. Any cough lasting longer than a few days or accompanied by weakness or difficulty breathing warrants a veterinary exam.

Does she have reddened or tearing eyes? Swelling and redness may indicate glaucoma, a scratched cornea, or several other problems. Profuse tear discharge may be caused by a foreign body, scratched cornea, or blocked tear drainage duct. Thick mucus and a dull-appearing surface may indicate "dry eye" (keratoconjunctivitis sicca, or KCS). Squinting or pawing at the eye can arise from pain. Dilated pupils with increased eye shine may be a sign of PRA (page 70).

Is she limping? Limping can arise from trauma, arthritis, or hereditary joint problems. Check the feet for cuts, abrasions, and overly long or split nails. Swollen toes could be from infection or an orthopedic problem. Many dogs suffer from tears of the knee's cruciate ligament, which may require surgery. Hip dysplasia and patellar luxation, both of which can cause lameness, are described on pages 72–74.

Is she scooting or licking her rear? Repeated diarrhea can cause an irritated anal area. Repeated scooting or licking can be from diarrhea, parasites, or, especially, impacted anal sacs. The anal sacs are two sacs filled with smelly brown liquid that normally is excreted with the feces or in times of fright. In some cases the material can't get out. The sac becomes uncomfortably distended, sometimes becoming infected. It may swell outward, even appearing to be a tumor, and often finally bursting. Your veterinarian can manually express the contents.

Medications

Giving medications to your Eskie should not be difficult.

Pills: For pills, open your dog's mouth and place (don't throw) the pill well to the back and in the middle of the tongue. Close the mouth and gently stroke the throat until your dog swallows. Beware that capsules often stick to the tongue or roof of the mouth; pre-wetting them or covering them with cream cheese or some other food may help.

Liquids: For liquid medicine, tilt the head back and place the liquid in the pouch of the cheek. Then close your dog's mouth until she swallows. Always give the full course of medications prescribed by your veterinarian.

When You Must Say Good-bye

Unfortunately, there comes the time when, no matter how diligent you have been, neither you nor your veterinarian can prevent your Eskie from succumbing to old age or an incurable illness. It seems hard to believe that you will have to say good-bye to someone who has been such a focal point of your life—in truth, a real member of your family. That dogs live such a short time compared to humans is a cruel fact, and as much as you may wish otherwise, your Eskie is a dog and is not immortal. You should realize that both of you have been fortunate to have shared so many good times, but make sure that your Eskie's remaining time is still pleasurable.

Many terminal illnesses make your dog feel very bad, and there comes a point when your desire to keep your friend with you as long as possible may not be the kindest thing for either of you. Ask your veterinarian if there is a reasonable chance of your dog getting better, and if she thinks your dog is suffering. Ask yourself if your dog is getting pleasure out of life, and if she enjoys most of her days. If your Eskie no longer eats her dinner or treats, this is a sign that she does not feel well and you must face the prospect of doing what is best for your beloved friend.

Euthanasia

Euthanasia is painless and involves giving an overdose of an anesthetic. If your dog is afraid of the veterinarian's office, you might feel better having the doctor meet you at home or come out to your car. Although it won't be easy, try to remain with your Eskie so that your friend's last moments will be filled with your love. Try to recall the wonderful times you have shared and realize that however painful it is losing such a once-in-a-lifetime dog, it is better than never having had such a friend in the first place.

You don't need a book to tell you how to love your dog, but there are some helpful hints when it comes to having fun with your dog.

So far, it might sound as though all that's involved in owning a dog is a whole lot of work. But millions of people would not own dogs if that were *all* there was to it!

The Great Outdoors— Safely

Use a collar that will not slip over your Eskie's head, a 6-foot (1.8-m) leather or nylon leash, or a longer retractable leash.

✔ Hold the leash firmly and never allow so much loose lead that your dog could jump in the path of a passing vehicle.

✔ Pick a regular time of day to walk and try to stick to it. Your Eskie will come to expect a walk at this time and won't fall for any excuses.

✔ Walk briskly so that you both can get a good workout. Trotting is usually best. If you wish your dog to jog with you, remember that dogs need to be worked up to long distances gradually, and be considerate of mini and toy Eskies.

Eskies are natural athletes.

✔ Check footpads regularly for abrasion, foreign bodies, tears, or blistering.

✔ Finally, leave your dog at home in hot weather. Dogs are unable to cool themselves through sweating, and so are vulnerable to heatstroke.

Running Off-Leash

✔ Never allow your friend to run loose in sight of traffic. Although your dog may usually stay with you, a cat, a rabbit, or another dog can lure your dog away and put him in danger.

✔ Never unhook the lead until you know everything about the area in which you will be walking. Is there a roadway around the next bend in the path? Dogs have been killed or injured by unseen peril.

✔ Watch out for strange dogs; some may not be friendly, and a little Eskie is no match for many of them.

✔ Once you know your area, be prepared for many wonderful times watching your friend run with wild abandon. Few things in life rival the look of sheer ecstasy in an Eskie's eyes as he reverts back to his roots and romps enthusiastically through nature.

Enclosed areas: You may fear that with such joy your dog may run away. For insurance, you should have practiced letting your dog run loose in enclosed areas and practiced the *come* command and used treats to ensure that your dog came every single time. You may even want to make sure that your dog is already hungry (and maybe a little tired) before you go if you have any doubts about his eager return.

Supplies: Pack some water and a little bowl for your dog. Also pack tape and bandages in case of a cut footpad. There may be some recreation that Eskies like better than hiking; however, it has yet to be discovered.

Hitting the Road

The small size, easygoing demeanor, and desire to be by their owner's side make Eskimo Dogs natural traveling companions. But consider that traveling with any dog limits where you can go. Many motels do not accept pets, and many attractions have no facilities for boarding. Most beaches, and many state parks, do not allow dogs. Dogs can no longer travel on trains. Several publications list motels and attractions that do accept dogs.

Sometimes the rules against dogs seem very unfair. Unfortunately, in many cases they are the only self-defense establishments have against irresponsible dog owners. Wherever you go, you will be scrutinized and upheld as an example of a typical dog owner.
✔ Don't let your dog defecate at will.
✔ Look for an appropriate route to walk your dog, then clean up after him.
✔ Don't leave your dog alone in a motel room. Loneliness and a strange room may cause your dog to bark, howl, or destroy the furniture.

✔ Don't let your dog chase wildlife at parks. Instead, go out of your way to do things properly, and perhaps, slowly, the tide may once again turn in favor of pets on the road.

Where Pets Are Welcome

Fortunately, there still remain some places where pets are welcome. Schedule several stops your Eskie can enjoy. If you are driving, bring a long retractable lead so your dog can stretch his legs safely every few hours along the way. Watch for nature excursions, which are refreshing for both dog and owner. But always do so with a cautious eye. Never let your Eskie off-lead in an unfamiliar spot.

Seat Belts

Ideally your Eskie should always ride with the equivalent of a doggy seat belt—the crate. Many dogs have emerged from their crates shaken but safe, from accidents that would have otherwise proved fatal.

Airlines

You will need an airline-approved crate if your Eskie must travel by air. Most Eskies will have to fly in a pressurized baggage compartment, but some small toy Eskies may be able to ride in the passenger section. Talk to an airline representative about facilities and requirements when you make reservations. Airlines will not generally allow dogs to be flown in extreme temperature conditions.

Flying dogs is relatively safe, but not entirely without risk, usually from overheating.
✔ Make sure the crate is secure, and put an elastic bungee around the door.
✔ Plaster your name and address all over the crate.

✔ Don't feed your dog before traveling. The crate should have a small dish that can be attached to the door. The night before the trip, fill it with water and freeze it; as it melts during the flight, the dog will have water that otherwise would have spilled out during the loading process. Also include a toy to occupy your traveler.

✔ Be sure to line the crate with soft, absorbent material, preferably something that can be thrown away if soiled.

✔ The flight crew should have been alerted that a dog is traveling, but it's wise to remind the flight attendant.

Arrival: When you arrive at your destination find out where to meet your friend; if flying excess baggage, your dog will arrive a little after the last of the regular baggage is distributed, but it is against regulations for live animals to be placed on baggage carousels. If your dog has not arrived by five minutes after the last baggage from your flight, inquire; if need be, become demanding. But in most cases bring your leash and be prepared for a joyous reunion!

Motels and visiting friends: Wherever you spend your nights, always have your dog on its best behavior.

✔ Ask beforehand if you can bring your Eskie.

✔ Have your dog clean and parasite-free.

✔ Do not allow your Eskie to run loose in public, and do not allow him to run through the homes of friends.

✔ Bring your dog's own crate. Your Eskie will appreciate the familiar place to sleep.

✔ Even though your dog may be used to sleeping on furniture at home, a proper guest dog stays on the floor when visiting.

✔ Walk and walk your dog (and clean up after him) to make sure no accidents occur inside. If

TIP

Car Sickness

Nothing can spoil the vision of you and your gleaming white puppy sharing a tranquil drive in the country like the reality of that puppy being covered with its own drool, or worse! Car sickness is a common ailment of puppies; most outgrow it, but some need car training in order to overcome it. Car rides should be made extremely short, with the object being to complete the ride before the dog gets sick. This may mean going only to the end of the driveway, and then working up to the end of the block.

Driving to a place where the dog can get out and enjoy himself before returning home also seems to help the dog look forward to car rides and overcome car sickness.

Motion sickness medication may be prescribed by your veterinarian to help in stubborn cases.

they do, clean them immediately. Don't leave any surprises for your hosts!

✔ Never leave your dog unattended in a strange place. The dog's perception is that you have abandoned him—he either barks or tries to dig his way out through doors and windows to find you, or becomes upset and relieves himself on the carpet.

Always remember that those who allow your dog to spend the night are doing so with some trepidation; make sure your Eskie is so well behaved that they invite you both back.

The Canine Good Citizen

Even if the only trip you take with your Eskie is around the block, please maintain the same high standards that you would if traveling.

✔ Always clean up after your dog. Carry a little plastic bag for disposal later.

✔ Don't let your dog run loose where he could be a nuisance.

✔ Never let your dog bark unchecked.

✔ Never let your dog jump up on people.

In order to formally recognize dogs that behave well in public, the AKC offers the Canine Good Citizen (CGC) certificate. To pass this test, your Eskie must demonstrate that he is well mannered in public. This means that he will walk quietly with you through a crowd, sit for examination, not jump up on, act aggressively toward, or shy away from someone who greets you, and stay in place without barking. The CGC is perhaps the most important title that your Eskie can earn. The most magnificent show dog is no credit to its breed if he is not a good public citizen in the real world.

Provisions: Pack a little suitcase for your dog as well as yourself; include your first aid kit, a bowl, some dog biscuits and chewies, flea spray, flea comb, a brush, a change of bedding, short and long leashes, and food. Besides the regular tags, your dog should wear identification indicating where you could be reached while on your trip or including the address of someone you know will be at home. If you are traveling by car, a jug of water from home can be a big help.

It may sound like a lot of work, but with a little preparation your Eskie can become a seasoned traveler, and you may wonder how you ever hit the road without him before.

Therapy Dogs

As more people become elderly and either unable to care for or keep a pet, the result is particularly sad for those who may have relied upon the companionship of a pet throughout most of their independent years. Studies have shown that pet ownership increases life expectancy and petting animals can lower blood pressure. In recent years, nursing home residents and hospitalized children have come to look forward to visits by dogs. These dogs must be meticulously well mannered and well groomed; to be registered as a Certified Therapy Dog a dog must demonstrate that he will be obedient, outgoing, and gentle to strangers. With his irresistible face and friendly, unassuming demeanor, the Eskie is a natural for this enjoyable, rewarding task.

Showing Off

Mind Games

Although routine obedience is necessary for good manners, it won't exactly astound your friends. For that you need something flashy, some incredible feat of intelligence and dexterity—a dog trick. Try the standards: roll over, play dead, catch, sit up, jump the stick, speak. All are easy to teach with the help of the same obedience concepts outlined in the training section (beginning on page 37).

Catch: Toss a morsel in the air above your dog's nose. When it hits the ground, pick it up.

Leap into action!

Eventually your Eskie will learn that he must grab the food before you do, and will snatch it up before it lands.

Speak: Most Eskies are easy to teach to "speak"; wait until it appears your dog will bark, say *"Speak,"* and then reward with a treat after the bark.

Roll over: A dog that likes to lie on his back is a natural for "roll over"; give the command when the dog is already on its back, then guide the dog the rest of the way over (and eventually over and over) with a treat.

If your dog can physically do a trick, you can teach him when to do it. Performing tricks enabled the American Eskimo Dog to work his way into American homes and hearts in the first place; today, Eskies don't need to be under a circus tent to work the same magic.

Obedience Trials

You plan on training your Eskie the *heel, sit, down, come,* and *stay* commands for use in everyday life. Add the *stand for exam* and your dog will have the basic skills necessary to earn the AKC Companion Dog (CD) title.

Each exercise has points assigned to it, and points are deducted for imperfections. In all but the *heel* commands, you can give a command only once, and in no cases can you touch, speak to, physically guide, correct, praise, or do anything except give the dog's name, followed by the command during that exercise. No food can be used. Your dog must pass each exercise and earn above the minimal 170 points to qualify. To earn the degree, he must qualify three times.

The UKC Companion Dog title (U-CD) requires much the same exercises, with the biggest dif-ference being that one dog is required to stay in the ring on a *down/stay* while another is doing its individual exercise.

Joining an obedience club will introduce you to others who will gladly give you training pointers and happily tell you that you have two left feet.

More advanced titles: In both AKC and UKC there are more advanced titles, where everything is done off-lead. The Companion Dog Excellent (CDX or U-CDX) also requires retrieving and jumping, and the even more advanced Utility Dog (UD or U-UD) requires hand signals and scent discrimination. Even with an Eskimo Dog, these titles take years of work. A UD is a rarity in most breeds, but Eskies boast several. The AKC Obedience Trial Champion (OTCH) degree is given only to dogs with UDs that outscore many other UD dogs in many, many trials. If you are at an obedience trial and see that an OTCH dog of any breed is entered, take the time to watch it go through its paces.

Agility

Perhaps no competitive event available for Eskies is more suited for this versatile breed, and certainly none is more loved by the dogs! Agility combines obedience, athleticism, and quickness, and is best suited for a medium-sized dog. Sound like any breed you know?

Dogs must negotiate a course of obstacles and jumps, including an A-frame, seesaw, elevated boardwalk, tunnels, and a variety of high and broad jumps (adjusted according to the height of the dog). There are Novice, Open, and Excellent classes, and the AKC awards, in increasing levels of difficulty, the titles Novice Agility Dog (NA), Open Agility Dog (OA), Agility Dog Excellent (AX), and Master Agility Champion (MACH). The UKC also offers challenging agility competitions and titles.

Flyball and Scent Hurdles

Both of these are relay races run with teams of four dogs that run down a course of four small jumps. In scent hurdle competition, the dog must then choose which of several articles belongs to his owner, and return with the correct one. Flyball competition also involves a course of jumps, but at the end of the course the dog then presses a treadle that pops a ball out of a box, catches the ball, and returns with it on the run to his owner.

Conformation

Conformation shows evaluate your Eskimo in comparison to the official breed standard. The judge examines each dog thoroughly, feeling his body structure beneath his coat, studying his movement, and viewing the total picture. If you find yourself admiring your dog around the yard, you may be interested in showing off in competition. The best place to start is by getting an honest opinion from your dog's breeder. As long as your Eskie has no disqualifying faults, you can show him. Of course, you may not win, but you will still learn a lot about the show world and be better prepared in the event that you would like to show your next Eskimo.

Training: To take the plunge, you must train your Eskie to pose and trot. The correct show pose is with all four paws pointing straight forward, legs parallel to each other and perpendicular to the ground, tail over the back, head and ears up. If your dog already knows the stand for exam, you have a head start. Reward the dog for keeping his feet where you place them, and for looking alert. In AKC shows you can use "bait" (typically boiled liver) to get the dog's attention in the ring, but even carrying bait into the show ring is against the rules at most UKC shows.

Practice trotting in a straight line, and encourage your dog to trot in a lively animated fashion. A happy attitude will overshadow many faults! The most common mistake new handlers make is to demand their dogs stand like statues for so long the poor dogs become bored. Professional handlers will show your dog for you and probably win more often than you would; however, nothing tops the thrill of winning when you do it yourself.

Contact your local kennel club or even obedience club and find out if they have handling classes, or when the next match will be held. Matches are informal events where everybody is learning: puppies, handlers, even the judges. Win or lose, never take one judge's opinion too seriously, and be polite.

Points: At a real AKC show, each time a judge chooses your dog as the best dog of his sex that is not already a Champion, he wins up to five points depending upon how many dogs he defeats. To become an AKC Champion your Eskie must win 15 points, including two majors (defeating enough dogs to win three to five points at a time). You may enter any class for which your dog is eligible: Puppy, 12–18 Months, Novice, American Bred, Bred by Exhibitor, or Open. The Best of Breed class is for dogs that are already Champions.

Rules and regulations (AKC): Your dog must be entered about three weeks before the show date, and you will need to get a premium list and entry form from the appropriate show superintendent (their addresses are available from the AKC).

Rules and regulations (UKC): At a UKC show, the atmosphere is more relaxed than at AKC shows. UKC shows can be entered the morning of the show; there are no superintendents, and all of the information necessary to enter can be found in the UKC publication *Bloodlines*. You must bring the dog's registration certificate and pedigree to enter. The requirements for a championship, too, are somewhat different. First, 100 points are needed. Classes for nonchampions are divided by age, sex, and variety, and the winner of each class receives five points, regardless of the number of dogs defeated. If he then wins best of his sex in that variety, he wins eight more points; best of his sex overall wins another ten

Exceptional Eskies

✔ The first (and, as of this writing, only) Eskie to achieve the supreme obedience title of Obedience Trial Champion is *CH OTCH Northrn Light Warp Factr Ten UDX NA NAJ*.

The first (and, as of this writing, only) Eskie to achieve the advanced tracking title Tracking Dog Excellent (TDX) is *CH Midnight Sun Solar Lone Star UD TDX VCD-3 MX MXJ*. Besides being a UKC Best in Show winner, Solar is the only Eskie to have the Versatile Companion Dog 3 (VCD-3) title, awarded to dogs with advanced titles in obedience, agility, and tracking.

✔ The first Eskie to earn an advanced agility title in any of the agility venues was *ADCH Chana*, who earned the title in the United States Dog Agility Association competition.

✔ The first Eskie to achieve the advanced agility title of Master Agility Champion (MACH) was the toy *MACH Ducat's Ruffian*. As of this writing there are 12 MACH Eskies.

✔ The first Eskie to achieve the advanced agility title of Master Agility Champion 2 is *CH MACH2 Anana Pikatti*. Pico is also the most titled Eskie, with 40 titles to his credit. The only other MACH2 Eskie is *Ch MACH2 Wysiwyg Kessona Li'l Loup-Loup*.

✔ The first Eskie with a Flyball Championship was *Rebel, FDCH*; the all-time top-winning flyball Eskie is *Ice, FMCH,* who is also the breed's first Flyball Master Champion (FMCH.)

points; and finally, best overall wins yet 12 more points. Once dogs become champions, they can compete against each other to earn the prestigious Grand Champion title.

ESKIE ESTHETICS

Every breed has a blueprint: a description of the ideal specimen.

No one dog ever fits the blueprint of the ideal specimen perfectly, but a dog should fit the standard well enough to be recognized as an American Eskimo Dog. This possession of breed attributes is known as type, and is important for any Eskie. A dog should also be built so it can go about its daily life with minimal exertion and without lameness. This equally important attribute is known as soundness. Add to these the attributes of good health and temperament, and you have the four cornerstones of the ideal American Eskimo Dog.

The Ideal American Eskimo Dog

Although the UKC standard and the AKC standard are worded differently, their essence is

A future champion?

the same, with only a few discrepancies. The largest discrepancy concerns the classification of sizes. UKC recognizes only two sizes: miniatures (males 12 to 15 inches [30.5–38.1 cm] inclusive and females 11 to 14 inches [27.9–35.6 cm] inclusive) and standards (males over 15 up to 19 inches [38.1–48.3 cm] and females over 14 up to 18 inches [35.6–45.7 cm]).

The AKC does not differentiate the sexes when considering size, but recognizes three different sizes: toys (9 to 12 inches [22.9–30.5 cm] inclusive), miniatures (over 12 up to 15 inches [30.5–38.1 cm]), and standards (over 15 up to 19 inches [38.1–48.3 cm]). Unlike the UKC, the AKC disqualifies dogs not meeting these height requirements.

The two standards describe ideal dogs having slightly different body proportions, with the UKC describing a basically square-bodied dog and the AKC describing one just slightly longer than tall. The AKC standard is more explicit in its descriptions of pastern slope, muzzle pro-

portions, toe shape, and pigment, specifically calling for white toenails and dark footpads. It also states that tearstains (unless severe) should not be faulted.

A note about nose color: Like many breeds, many Eskies will get a "winter nose," meaning that the nose pigment gets lighter during the winter months.

The AKC Standard

Following are the main points of the AKC standard. The complete standard can be found at the National Club Web sites or at *www.akc.org*.

"The American Eskimo Dog . . . presents a picture of strength and agility, alertness and beauty."

General Appearance

The American Eskimo Dog, a loving companion dog, presents a picture of strength and agility, alertness and beauty. It is a small to medium-size Nordic type dog, always white, or white with biscuit cream. The American Eskimo Dog is compactly built and well balanced, with good substance, and an alert, smooth gait. The face is Nordic type with erect triangular shaped ears, and distinctive black points (lips, nose, and eye rims). The white double coat consists of a short, dense undercoat, with a longer guard hair growing through it forming the outer coat, which is straight with no curl or wave. The coat is thicker and longer around the neck and chest forming a lion-like ruff, which is more noticeable on dogs than on bitches. The rump and hind legs down to the hocks are also covered with thicker, longer hair forming the characteristic breeches. The richly plumed tail is carried loosely on the back.

Size, Proportion, Substance

Size: There are three separate size divisions of the American Eskimo Dog (all measurements are heights at withers): Toy, 9 inches to and including 12 inches; Miniature, over 12 inches to and including 15 inches; and Standard, over 15 inches to and including 19 inches. There is no preference for size within each division. *Disqualification: Under 9 inches or over 19 inches. Proportion.* Length of back from point of shoulder to point of buttocks is slightly greater than height at withers, an approximate 1.1 to 1 ratio. *Substance.* The American Eskimo

TIP

Standard Definitions

✔ **Withers:** Highest point of the shoulder.

✔ **Stop:** Transition point from forehead to muzzle, as viewed in profile.

✔ **Scissors bite:** The back surface of the top incisors meet the front surface of the bottom incisors when the mouth is closed.

✔ **Topline:** The line from the neck to the tail, viewed in silhouette.

✔ **Angulated:** Refers to the angles formed between the shoulder blade and the humerus in the forequarters, and the pelvis, thigh, and knee in the rearquarters. Well-angulated requires these angles to be close to 90 degrees.

✔ **Point of hock:** Anatomical correlate to the human heel.

✔ **Coupled:** Area between the rib cage and the rearquarters.

✔ **Trot:** Gait where diagonal legs move in unison.

✔ **Pace:** Gait where legs on the same side of the body move in unison.

The expression is keen, alert, and intelligent.

Dog is strong and compactly built with adequate bone.

Coat

The American Eskimo Dog has a stand-off, double coat consisting of a dense undercoat and a longer coat of guard hair growing through it to form the outer coat. It is straight with no curl or wave. There is a pronounced ruff around the neck which is more noticeable on dogs than bitches. Outer part of the ear should be well covered with short, smooth hair, with longer tufts of hair growing in front of ear openings. Hair on muzzle should be short and smooth. The backs of the front legs should be well feathered, as are the rear legs down to the hock. The tail is covered profusely with long hair. THERE IS TO BE NO TRIMMING OF THE WHISKERS OR BODY COAT AND SUCH TRIMMING WILL BE SEVERELY PENALIZED. The only permissible trimming is to neaten the feet and the backs of the rear pasterns.

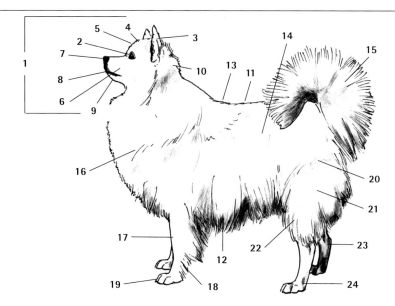

1 Expression: keen, intelligent, and alert.

2 Eyes: set well apart; slightly oval, but not slanted, prominent or bulging. Eye color dark to medium brown. Tearstain, unless severe, is not to be faulted. Faults: amber eye color or pink eye rims. Disqualification: blue eyes.

3 Ears: erect, set on high yet well apart; triangular with slightly blunt tips.

4 Skull: slightly crowned and softly wedge-shaped; widest between the ears.

5 Stop: well-defined, although not abrupt.

6 Muzzle: broad, with length not exceeding the length of the skull.

7 Nose: black to dark brown. *Fault: pink nose pigment.*

8 Lips: thin and tight, black to dark brown in color. *Fault: pink lip pigment.*

9 Jaw: strong, with a full complement of close fitting teeth and scissors bite.

10 Neck: medium in length, carried erect in a strong, graceful arch.

11 Topline: level.

12 Chest: Extends approximately to point of elbows, with well-sprung ribs. Slight tuck-up of belly just behind the ribs.

13 Back: straight, broad, level, and muscular.

14 Loin: strong and well-muscled.

15 Tail: set moderately high and carried loosely on the back; may be dropped when at rest, reaching approximately to the point of hock.

16 Forequarters: well angulated. Shoulder blade slants 45° with the horizontal and forms an approximate right angle with the upper arm.

17 Forelegs: parallel and straight to the pasterns.

18 Pasterns: strong and flexible with a slant of about 20°. Dewclaws may or may not be removed.

19 Feet: oval, compact, and well padded with hair. Toes are well arched. Pads are black to dark brown, tough, and deeply cushioned. Toenails are white.

20 Hindquarters: well angulated; the lay of the pelvis is approximately 30° to the horizontal.

21 Upper thigh: well developed.

22 Stifle: well bent.

23 Hock joint: well let down and firm. The rear pasterns are straight.

24 Hind legs: parallel from the rear and turn neither in nor out. Dewclaws are not present on the hind legs.

No dog is perfect, but the best examples of the breed will conform to the standard as closely as possible.

Color

Pure white is the preferred color, although white with biscuit cream is permissible. Presence of biscuit cream should not outweigh consideration of type, structure, or temperament. The skin of the American Eskimo Dog is pink or gray. *Disqualification: any color other than white or biscuit cream.*

Gait

The American Eskimo Dog shall trot, not pace. The gait is agile, bold, well balanced, and frictionless, with good forequarter reach and good hindquarter drive. As speed increases, the American Eskimo Dog will single track with the legs converging toward the center line of gravity while the back remains firm, strong, and level.

Temperament

The American Eskimo Dog is intelligent, alert, and friendly, although slightly conservative. It is never overly shy nor aggressive, and such dogs are to be severely penalized in the show ring. At home it is an excellent watchdog, sounding a warning bark to announce the arrival of any stranger. It is protective of its home and family, although it does not threaten to bite or attack people. The American Eskimo Dog learns new tasks quickly and is eager to please.

Disqualifications

Any color other than white or biscuit cream
Blue eyes
Height: under 9" or over 19"

INFORMATION

Organizations

American Kennel Club
51 Madison Avenue
New York, NY 10038
212-696-8200
www.akc.org

For registration information:
American Kennel Club
5580 Centerview Drive
Raleigh, NC 27606
919-233-9767

United Kennel Club
100 East Kilgore Road
Kalamazoo, MI 49001-5598
616-343-9020
www.ukcdogs.com

American Eskimo Dog Club of America (AKC)*
Lynn McClure
3242 S. 187th Street
Seatac, WA 98188
(206) 242-9944
http://mywebpages.comcast.net/jamarsch/aedca/

National American Eskimo Dog Association
  (UKC)*
Debbie Mitchell
11994 Pruett Road
Krum, TX 76249
(940) 482-3699
http://www.eskie.com/naeda/

National American Eskimo Dog Association
  of Canada
http://naedac.topcities.com/

*This address or phone number may change with the election of new officers. The current listing can be obtained by contacting the American Kennel Club.

Other National All-breed Clubs
http://henceforths.com/kennel_clubs.html

Regional American Eskimo Dog Clubs
*http://www.netpets.com/dogs/dogclub/breeds/
  dogaesk.html*

Health Organizations

American College of Veterinary
  Ophthalmologists
www.acvo.org

Canine Eye Registration Foundation
Purdue University
CERF/Lynn Hall
625 Harrison Street
West Lafayette, IN 47907-2026
(765) 494-8179
http://www.vet.purdue.edu/~yshen/cerf.html

Canine Health Foundation
http://akcchf.org

Optigen
Cornell Business & Technology Park
767 Warren Road, Suite 300
Ithaca, New York 14850
(607) 257-0301
www.optigen.com

Orthopedic Foundation for Animals
2300 Nifong Boulevard
Columbia, MO 65201
http://www.offa.org

Rescue

Eskie Rescuers United
P.O. Box 61
Belle Chasse, LA 70037
http://www.eskierescuers.org/

NAEDA Rescue Coordinator
Kim Galloway
(770) 963-6120 (calls will be returned collect)
Sunshadows@charter.net

Heart Bandits
P.O. Box 4322
Fresno, CA 93744-4322
(559) 299-6729
http://www.heartbandits.com/

Periodicals
Dog World Magazine
www.dogworldmag.com

Animal Network
http://www.animalnetwork.com

Books
Benyon, Barbara. *The Complete American Eskimo: A Special Kind of Companion.* New York: Howell, 1990.
Coile, D. Caroline. *Beyond Fetch: Fun, Interactive Activities for You and Your Dog.* New York: Wiley, 2003.
——. *Show Me! A Dog Showing Primer.* Hauppauge, NY: Barron's Educational Series, 1997.
Hofman, Nancy, and Cathy Flamholtz. *The New American Eskimo.* Ft. Payne, AL: OTR Publications, 1996.
Sellers, Monica. *American Eskimos.* Neptune City, NJ: TFH, 1997.

NAEDA Pre-2000 UKC Titlist Handbook
NAEDA 2000 UKC Titlist Handbook
NAEDA 2001/2002 UKC Titlist Handbook
NAEDA 2003/2004 UKC Titlist Handbook
Order from: Kathy Kozakiewicz
2739 N 21 Drive
Phoenix, AZ 85009
kistari@cox.net

Videos
AKC Breed Standard Video
http://www.akc.org/store/

Web Pages
American Eskimo
http://www.americaneskimo.com/

Animal CPR
http://members.aol.com/henryhbk/acpr.html

Infodog Dog Show site
http://www.infodog.com

Eskie Central
http://www.eskie.net/central/

Eskie Friends
http://www.eskiefriends.com/

Eskies Online
http://www.eskiesonline.com/

K9Info breed and pedigree source
http://www.k9info.com

Lost Pet Information
http://lostpet.org/missing_dogs.html

The Dog Agility Page
http://www.dogpatch.org/agility/

Dr. P's Dog Training Links
http://www.uwsp.edu/acad/psych/dog/dog.htm

Therapy Dogs International
http://www.tdi-dog.org

Cover Credits

Paulette Braun: front cover, back cover, and inside front cover and Kent Dannen: inside back cover.

About the Author

Caroline Coile is an award-winning author who has written articles about dogs for both scientific and lay publications. She holds a Ph.D. in the field of neuroscience and behavior, with special interests in canine sensory systems, genetics, and behavior. Her own dogs have been nationally ranked in conformation, obedience, and field-trial competition.

Acknowledgments

The author is indebted to American Eskimo Dog breeders Sally Bedow, Carolyn Jester, Emily Johnson, and Kathy Kozakiewicz for their valuable contributions to the text. Special thanks to Barron's senior editor Seymour Weiss.

Important Note

This pet owner's manual tells the reader how to buy or adopt, and care for, an American Eskimo Dog. The author and publisher consider it important to point out that the advice given in the book is meant primarily for normally developed dogs of excellent physical health and sound temperament.

Anyone who acquires a fully grown dog should be aware that the animal has already formed its basic impressions of human beings. The new owner should watch the animal carefully, including its behavior toward humans, and, whenever possible, should meet the previous owner.

Caution is further advised in the association of children with dogs, in meeting with other dogs, and in exercising the dog without a leash.

Even well-behaved and carefully supervised dogs sometimes do damage to someone else's property or cause accidents. It is therefore in the owner's interest to be adequately insured against such eventualities, and we strongly urge all dog owners to purchase a liability policy that covers their dog.

Photo Credits

Norvia Behling: 4, 7, 38, 51, and 65; Paulette Braun: 2–3, 10, 14, 20, 45, 50, 56, 58, 60, 64, 67, 73, and 91; Kent Dannen: 5, 11, 21, 23, 24, 27, 28, 30, 31, 34, 36, 37, 46, 61, 69, 71, 86, 87, 88, and 89; Tara Darling: 19 (top), 42, 53, and 57; Cheryl Ertelt: 52; Diane Lewis: 8, 19 (bottom), 33, 76, 77, 78, and 83; and Judith Strom: 43 and 44.

All inquiries should be addressed to:
Barron's Educational Series, Inc.
250 Wireless Boulevard
Hauppauge, NY 11788
www.barronseduc.com

ISBN-13: 978-0-7641-2861-5
ISBN-10: 0-7641-2861-2

Library of Congress Catalog Card No. 2005043014

Library of Congress Cataloging-in-Publication Data
Coile, D. Caroline.
    American Eskimo dogs : everything about purchase, care, nutrition, behavior, and training / D. Caroline Coile ; illustrations by Michele Earle-Bridges.
        p. cm.
    Includes bibliographical references and index.
    ISBN 0-7641-2861-2
    1. American Eskimo dog. I. Title.

SF429.A69C65   2005
636.73—dc22   2005043014

Printed in China
9 8 7 6 5 4 3 2 1